7096

CAREERS IN LAW
ENFORCEMENT
AND SECURITY

CAREERS IN LAW ENFORCEMENT AND SECURITY

By
PAUL COHEN
and
SHARI COHEN

The Rosen Publishing Group, Inc.
NEW YORK

Published in 1990, 1995 by The Rosen Publishing Group, Inc.
29 East 21st Street, New York, NY 10010

Revised Edition 1995

Library of Congress Cataloging-in-Publication Data

Cohen, Paul, 1948
   Careers in law enforcement and security / by Paul Cohen and Shari Cohen. — rev. ed.
     p.   cm.
   Summary: Discusses career possibilities as private investigators, police, and in the field of law enforcement.
   Includes bibliographical references.
   ISBN 0-8239-1878-5; 0-8239-1908-0 (pbk.)
   1. Police—Vocational guidance—United States—Juvenile literature.   2. Law enforcement—Vocational guidance—United States—Juvenile literature. [1. Private investigators—Vocational guidance.   2. Police—Vocational guidance.   3. Law enforcement—Vocational guidance.   4. Vocational guidance.]   I. Cohen, Shari. II. Title.
HV7922.C64   1990   90-8063
363.2'023';73—dc20   CIP
                                        AC

Manufactured in the United States of America

About the Authors

Paul Cohen is a native of Milwaukee, Wisconsin. After graduating from the University of Wisconsin, he and his wife, Shari, moved to Los Angeles, where he attended law school. After earning a J.D. degree in law, he opened his own investigation business, Cohen & Associates, in 1976.

Paul works closely with attorneys and insurance companies, bringing in witnesses and gathering facts and information for various cases. Cohen & Associates is often called upon to assist in newsworthy court trials throughout the nation.

Shari Cohen also has an investigation license through the state of California. She assists Paul in the daily operations of Cohen & Associates. Shari is the author of six books and is currently involved in writing and developing stories for television.

The Cohens live in Woodland Hills, California, with their three children, Barry, Adam, and Stephanie.

Contents

Introduction

Movies today usually depict members of the law-enforcement field as tough, brooding loners who can outwit any criminal they encounter. Whether male or female, private detective, police officer, or FBI agent, these officials possess a brilliance of both mind and body that is difficult to imagine in real life. They out-maneuver gangs of criminals using techniques borrowed from karate masters. They capture drug dealers and mass murderers with unbelievable ease, and they do it all with a quick sense of humor and a ready smile.

Movies from the past offer different, yet still un-realistic, images. Private detectives of the 1950s were played by middle-aged men who wore raincoats and slanted hats. These characters chain-smoked cigarettes, talked in rough, gravelly voices, and always got the bad guy in the end. In the 1970s and 1980s, the law-enforcement officials were represented by the Magnum and Rockford types—tall, good-looking guys who carried guns and lived in remote houses close to the beach. The characters in "Law and Order" and "NYPD Blue" in the '90s come closer to the realities of law enforcers but still mange to conclude cases within a remarkably short time.

These images portray the law-enforcement field in a way that makes it seem unattainable to "average" people. The movie "good guys" are superhuman; most of us are not. Careers in law enforcement in real life, however, are open to people who are not superhuman. Police officers, federal agents, and other enforcers of the law are hard-working, law-abiding people. They include men and women of all nationalities and backgrounds.

Many work long hours and investigate a case for years before it is solved.

This book discusses career opportunities in the law-enforcement field, including work in police departments, the Federal Bureau of Investigation (FBI), the Central Intelligence Agency (CIA), and the Secret Service. The book also describes detective work, drug-enforcement jobs and security guard careers. In addition to descriptions of the various careers, it provides personal interviews with a number of people serving in law enforcement and other related occupations.

Deciding whether or not a law-enforcement career is right for you will take time and patience. You must be honest with yourself and try to identify your strengths and weaknesses, your interests and dislikes. Once you have decided on law enforcement, choosing one of the jobs in the field may take even more time. This book will help you begin your research into a field that many people find both rewarding and challenging.

1

How the System Works

No society could exist without laws. Laws tell us what we can and cannot do. Laws tell us how fast we can drive our cars and where and when we can park them. Laws define the age at which we can drink alcohol, when we can vote, and when we must pay taxes. Without laws people could do anything they pleased, without regard for the rights of others. Laws are written and changed as the needs of society change.

In the United States, and in most societies, police agencies and courts make sure the laws are obeyed. Police officers are enforcers of our laws. They protect us by making sure that others abide by the laws. Imagine how different life would be without laws or police. Cities everywhere would be filled with violence. We would all have to defend ourselves against the criminals. No one would be arrested or spend time in jail. Thieves and murderers would roam the towns, and it would literally be war on our streets.

Law enforcers keep order in communities, states, or countries. They enforce the law so that people can live together peaceably. Police officers are trained to know the law and enforce it. They prevent crime and protect lives and property. In the United States, police agencies operate under the city, county, state, and federal governments. Each agency is responsible to its own division of government.

A police agency contains many careers you could choose. When you think of police, you probably visualize the officers you see handling patrol and traffic operations. These are the most visible members of police agencies. Patrol officers are assigned to cover a particular area on foot, in squad cars, on motorcycles, and sometimes even on horseback or on bicycles. Traffic officers direct traffic, assist stranded motorists, enforce parking laws, and make sure the speed limit is observed.

Other police officials include detectives, undercover agents, juvenile officers, and records and communications officials. Some policemen and policewomen are members of search and rescue teams, hostage negotiating teams, bomb squads, and special weapons units. The following is a breakdown of the various areas of law enforcement and a brief description of their duties and responsibilities.

City Police

City police have the power to enforce the law within their own city limits. In some states, under special circumstances city officers can exercise their police powers in other communities. Other states allow city police to exercise their powers throughout the state.

The size of a city police force depends on the size and the needs of the community. Small town police forces have only a couple of officers. Cities like New York, which has the largest city police department in the United States, have more than 20,000 officers.

Each police department's goal is to prevent crime, investigate crime, and apprehend offenders. The police also work to control traffic, handle crowd control, and deal with emergencies and disasters. In addition, police officers may perform the following duties:

- patrol areas and make observations
- answer emergency calls
- conduct investigations
- write reports
- testify in court.

City police who are assigned to patrol a particular area (a beat) are on the lookout for stolen automobiles, suspicious characters, or odd circumstances. Patrol officers may receive assignments from headquarters over a radio that they carry on their person or in their car. A dispatch officer sends out assignments over the radio. Officers then investigate the reported crime or disturbance.

County Police

The powers of a county police force extend throughout the county, except into towns and cities that have their own police force. A sheriff, elected by the people, is the chief law-enforcement officer in most counties. In some states the sheriff's department provides services on a contract basis to cities and towns within the county.

The sheriff's duties vary from one county to the next. The department may be responsible for all traffic procedures or for prisoners in the county jails. It may even be involved in settling business disputes and other civil matters. The sheriff's department also conducts certain police operations and provides training and local services to city police.

State Police

State police enforce state laws. Every state, except Hawaii, has a state police force or a state highway patrol force. State highway patrol officers, sometimes called state troopers, enforce highway and motor vehicle regulations. They enforce traffic laws, issue traffic tickets

3

to motorists who violate those laws, provide information to travelers, handle traffic control, and summon emergency equipment at the scene of an accident. Sometimes state highway patrol officers check the weight of commercial vehicles and conduct driver's tests.

Members of a state police force often perform the same duties as the state highway patrol. In addition to these duties, state police may coordinate police activities throughout a state and provide training to city and county police officers.

California has the largest number of state police; North Dakota has the smallest. In Hawaii, instead of state police, only county police forces are used.

FEDERAL LAW ENFORCEMENT

Ten major federal law enforcement agencies have full police powers. They collect taxes and enforce constitutional and federal laws. The agencies include:

- Federal Bureau of Investigation
- Immigration and Naturalization Service
- Drug Enforcement Administration
- U.S. Marshals Service
- Postal Inspection Service
- U.S. Secret Service
- Internal Revenue Service
- U.S. Customs Service
- Bureau of Alcohol, Tobacco and Firearms
- U.S. Coast Guard

These agencies are governed by the Department of Justice, the Department of Treasury, or the U.S. Postal Service.

Federal Bureau of Investigation

The FBI is the principal investigative arm of the U.S. Department of Justice. Members of the FBI gather and

4

report facts, locate witnesses, and compile evidence in cases under federal jurisdiction. Bureau investigators deal with bank robberies and kidnapping, investigate violations of federal law, and provide training, identification, and laboratory services to local police.

United States Marshals Service
The U.S. Marshals Service is the oldest federal law-enforcement agency in the nation. The Marshals Service is responsible for tasks that involve the federal justice system. Its members provide support and protection for the federal courts, including the security of judicial facilities, judges, jurors, attorneys, and other trial participants; apprehend most federal fugitives; operate the Federal Witness Security program; transport federal prisoners, and execute court orders and warrant arrests. The Marshals Service is in the U.S. Department of Justice.

Immigration and Naturalization Service
The INS has the dual mission of providing information and service to the general public and exercising enforcement responsibilities. Members of the INS enforce laws regarding immigrants or visitors to the United States, prevent unlawful entry of aliens, and remove those who enter the United States illegally. The INS is in the U.S. Department of Justice.

Drug Enforcement Administration
The DEA enforces laws governing narcotics and controlled substances. Its members present cases to the justice systems regarding the growing, smuggling, or distribution of drugs. The DEA arrests drug dealers and smugglers, confiscates drugs, and tries to reduce the amount of controlled substances available. The Drug

Enforcement Administration is governed by the Department of Justice.

Bureau of Alcohol, Tobacco and Firearms

Established by the Treasury Department, the BATF is headquartered in Washington, but most of its personnel live throughout the United States. They are responsible for enforcing the firearms and explosives laws. Some of the duties of Bureau employees are investigating bombings, identifying tax violations related to alcohol and tobacco, and suppressing the illegal possession and use of firearms.

U.S. Customs Service

Officials of the U.S. Customs Service collect duties on imported goods and materials. They also seize contraband materials, including illegal drugs. The Customs Service is governed by the Department of Treasury and is headquartered in Washington.

U.S. Secret Service

Members of the Secret Service protect the President of the United States, the Vice-President, the President-elect, the Vice-President-elect and members of their immediate families. Secret Service officials also protect major Presidential and Vice-Presidential candidates, former Presidents, and their spouses. Secret Service employees also investigate forgery or counterfeiting schemes. The Secret Service is overseen by the Department of Treasury.

U.S. Coast Guard

The U.S. Coast Guard is a component of the Department of Transportation. Coast Guard employees perform a number of duties, including search and rescue, maritime law enforcement, marine inspection, marine licensing, port safety and security, boating safety, military readiness, and reserve training. In time of war it functions as part of the U.S. Navy.

Postal Inspection Service

The Postal Inspection Service is the law-enforcement arm of the U.S. Postal Service. Duties of its employees include protecting the mail, postal funds, and property; investigating internal conditions and needs that may affect postal security; apprehending violators of postal laws, and auditing finances.

Internal Revenue Service

The IRS collects tax revenues. Its members encourage voluntary compliance with tax laws, identify those who violate tax laws, and provide taxpayer service and education. The IRS is overseen by the Department of Treasury.

Private Police Agencies

Private police agencies are licensed by the state to perform limited types of police work. Industrial security police guard factories and warehouses. Campus police are hired to protect the people and property of colleges and universities. Private investigative agencies provide detective services to individuals and businesses.

2

Careers in Police Work—City, County, and State

The duties of a police officer depend to a large extent on the size of the town or city in which he or she works. Officers in small towns have a wider range of duties than those in large cities. City police departments have many divisions, each of which has squads of officers who do specialized work.

A typical police department includes police chief (the highest ranking officer), commander (second in charge), captain, lieutenants, sergeants, and police officers.

POLICE DEPARTMENT CAREER LADDER

Chief

|

Deputy Chief

|

Commander

|

Captain

|

Lieutenant

|

Sergeant

|

Police Officer

The *commissioner, chief of police,* or *superintendent* is the executive head of the department. This person usually is appointed by the mayor, city administrator, or legislative body. In larger agencies, executive officers may be selected through a Civil Service merit system, after moving up through the ranks from patrol officer.

A *captain* typically is the commanding officer of a specific area or division. The captain position is regarded as the entry administrative position.

The *lieutenant* usually is a watch commander in a large geographical area or the officer-in-charge of a particular section of the police department. A lieutenant is a supervisor, like the sergeant, but he or she has broader administrative responsibilities.

Sergeants are field supervisors. They also have administrative and special assignments, but the focus of their job is to supervise the field.

An *officer* can be promoted after a specified length of service and after meeting certain requirements. Promotion ranges from officer grade three to grade two and grade one. After becoming a police officer grade one, you could be promoted to sergeant, then lieutenant, then captain and higher.

PATROL OFFICERS

Patrol officers work in assigned sections (beats) of a city. They may patrol their area in marked police cars, on foot, on horseback, or on bicycles. Horses and bicycles usually are used only in larger cities. But whatever their mode of transportation, the uniformed officers in the patrol division provide basic police services.

Although much of a patrol officer's work involves handling minor complaints, such as family disputes and arguing neighbors, in many instances these calls can erupt into major situations. A case of domestic bickering can escalate into a violent or abusive argument. A report

9

of a crying child can lead to the discovery of child abuse. Every call a patrol officer receives is important and must be investigated thoroughly. Officers who answer these calls must be professionally trained to handle a variety of situations. They must always be alert and able to analyze quickly what is happening around them.

"One thing a rookie quickly finds out is that the policeman is a jack-of-all-trades," says Fred J. Cook in his book *City Cop*. "If there is a family dispute, we are almost certain to be called. We try to keep the husband and wife from killing each other. We act like lawyers in the case, questioning first one, then the other, to find out what has caused the trouble. Then we try to act as marriage counselors, to get the couple calmed down and on friendly terms—for the time being, at least."

Take the case of Brian and Paul, two police officers working the night shift in Minneapolis. Like all officers, these two often are called upon to perform several emergency duties at the same time. This might be a typical evening:

After coming on duty at midnight, Brian and Paul arrested a drunk driver, broke up a major street gang fight, then stopped for a break. While on the break, they received a call about a possible fire in a home just a few blocks away.

Brian and Paul arrived on the scene minutes later and saw that it was indeed a fire and that the fire was out of control. The lower floor of a two-story home was in flames. People were panicking, there were injuries to attend to, and two men were fleeing into a back alley. Brian attended to the injured and summoned the police department and the paramedics. Paul set off to capture the men, who were suspected of arson.

Smoke continued to billow out of the house, and Brian was told by the homeowner that his dog was still inside. The fire trucks had not yet arrived, so Brian waited for an chance to go into the house. Struggling to hold his breath, Brian ran inside and searched for the German shepherd. The heat in the living room was intense, and Brian doubted that the dog was still alive. Suddenly he heard a whimper coming from a back room. He made his way through the smoke and found the dog curled up next to a bed, struggling for air. Brian grabbed the dog by the collar and, because of its weight, dragged it to the front door and out to safety.

Meanwhile, Paul was chasing the two suspects down the alley and over a fence. He finally cornered them and they gave up, raising their hands. Paul walked them back to the house.

By this time, the fire department and paramedics were on the scene, and back-up police had arrived to assist the two officers. The situation was under control, and Brian and Paul were finally able to leave the site.

Emergency Calls

Many of the calls handled by patrol officers are 911 emergency calls. When an officer responds to an emergency call, every minute of delay could be a matter of life and death. Quick response is a key to service, but the officer must use both speed and caution when answering a 911 call.

In some cities, police use "hotshot cars" that respond only to the most serious of the priority-one calls. The hotshot car system allows police to respond to life-threatening situations even before other emergency calls. At these scenes, the patrol officer is the one who is called upon to save someone from drowning or to prevent someone from bleeding to death.

The Scene of a Crime

Officers who are the first to arrive at any crime scene have responsibilities in addition to helping the victims and apprehending the perpetrators. One of these is locating and preserving evidence.

An officer is in action from the moment he or she arrives at the scene. Identifying evidence might require that an officer slow down long enough to find out:

- How did this situation come about?
- What evidence is left here at the scene?
- How can this area be protected from the public until others in the department arrive?

A hair or a bloodstain found at the scene can be collected and sent to the lab for inspection. Even the smallest piece of evidence can make a world of difference if the case comes to trial. That single hair, for example, may be enough to convict a person of the crime. So an officer must notice every minute detail and act as an investigator in collecting the facts and evidence.

A report is written on the spot and includes the officer's personal comments. At a later date that report and the evidence collected may be used by police detectives or FBI investigators. The officer may have to testify in court about the evidence and about the scene as he or she found it upon arrival. To do all this efficiently, patrol officers must rely on their skills and training to recognize and safeguard evidence.

Frustrations and Triumphs

One of the frustrations of working as a police officer is the inability to help victims of a crime or an accident. In a drowning or a murder, an officer may arrive on the scene too late. Says one officer:

"I've had people die in my arms. It's not always easy to play the macho part, to be strong and unmoved. I know there is nothing I can do to help them, but it's a forceful feeling. Even the ones who deserve it . . . they become just another human being who is on the way out. I sometimes think that they could be family or a friend, and I hate to admit it but I've shed some tears right along with them. I try to hold the emotions in check and save them for later, but when a guy or kid is taking his last breath, you forget about the image. The image means nothing when a brother is saying his last goodbye."

Most crime calls are answered, not by the superhuman police officers you see in movies, but by experienced, hard-working men and women. Often these men and women become frustrated dealing with situations in which a criminal gets away or a crime goes unsolved. At times there may seem to be nothing but bloodshed, murder, or theft.

But there are triumphs, too, and these balance out the frustrations. There are days when a lost child is reunited with her parents, a bomb is located and dismantled, a baby is delivered safely at home. There are triumphs and frustrations in every day of a police officer's life. It is for the triumphs that an officer remains dedicated to his or her job. Being a good patrol officer requires this dedication, hard work, and an understanding that some tragedies cannot be avoided, no matter how hard you try.

TRAFFIC OFFICERS

Traffic officers have a variety of duties. They observe drivers and make sure that speed and safety laws are obeyed. They direct traffic at intersections. They study traffic codes and violations. Traffic officers are also trained to perform cardiopulmonary resuscitation (CPR).

Many traffic officers answer emergency calls about accidents. When an officer arrives at the scene of an accident, he or she has a number of duties. The officer learns if anyone is injured. If there are injuries, a paramedic or an ambulance is summoned, and the officer administers emergency first aid until other help arrives.

It is the officer's responsibility to set warning flares around the accident scene so that passersby will not interfere. The officer must observe the incident and write a report on the spot. Notations are made of the existence of skid marks or the position of the vehicle or vehicles after impact. A sketch or diagram is made of the scene as it was when the officer arrived: the direction in which the vehicles were traveling, where the point of impact occurred, etc.

A traffic officer can arrest a driver if the officer is sure or even suspects that the driver caused the accident because of drunkenness or drugs or another cause. The officer helps get the situation under control and then follows the victim(s) to the hospital. There, if possible, the officer talks with all the injured parties. The officer may ask some of the following questions:

- Whose fault was the accident?
- In what direction were the cars moving?

14

- Did the other driver signal before turning or striking?
- Was one of the drivers speeding?

The officer completes a preliminary investigation and later files a complete report at headquarters. The report will be referred to at a later date, either by insurance companies or by attorneys who may be filing a lawsuit. The officer's notations are important and may make a great difference in a person's driving record and insurance status.

Traffic officers must be able to work in a variety of weather conditions. They may find themselves working in the worst snowstorm of the century or in a torrential rainstorm. It may be icy cold or stiflingly hot.

A traffic officer's job can be tedious one day, stopping people for a broken taillight or an invalid registration. The next day, though, may bring a major collision at a heavily traveled intersection. Good officers must be prepared for both kinds of days and any kind of weather whenever they are on duty.

COMMUNICATIONS OFFICER

A communications officer, or dispatcher, alerts officers in the field about emergency situations or possible criminal activity. A dispatcher is assigned to and stays in continual radio contact with the officers who patrol a particular city area. Dispatchers work at a computer console and direct their officers to traffic or other problems as they occur. They supply the officers with information about problem situations, whether they be accidents or domestic disputes or robberies.

Calls to dispatchers come in to computer panel boards at police headquarters. Each board shows a map of a portion of the city. Squad cars are shown on the board as white dots; red dots are the cars of police supervisors.

The communications operators can see the location of every police car at any moment of the day or night. When a call comes in, it is immediately directed to the operator whose board covers that area. The communications officer coordinates all moves from his or her board.

MARINE OFFICERS

Cities near bodies of water often employ marine officers to patrol a particular area in motorboats or launches. These officers watch wharf areas, coves, and piers for signs of criminal activity, such as theft, vandalism, or arson. They also assist boaters in distress or people in trouble along the waterway.

JUVENILE OFFICERS

All officers come into contact with juveniles while on the job. A juvenile may be the crime victim or the criminal. The typical juvenile case comes to police attention when an officer on a beat observes criminal acts done by a juvenile. A separate group of officers handle such cases; they are called juvenile officers.

Juvenile officers must have a knowledge of social work and an understanding of child psychology. That combination of skills is most likely to be found in a person trained as a psychiatric social worker. Many juvenile offenders come from troubled homes and have received little or no help in dealing with their problems. Juvenile officers need the extra training to work more productively with juvenile offenders.

Juvenile officers analyze the case to which they are assigned and try to interview school personnel, parents, and friends of the family. They look at motivating factors, such as serious problems at home or school, or drug or alcohol abuse. The information gathered is organized into a report for the court; it assists those who later must make decisions about an offender's future.

Many divisional detectives handle juvenile crimes that occur at any time, day or night. The officers encounter a variety of incidents, such as robbery, homicide, and sexual assault. After arrests are made, officers often talk to the offender's parents and recommend courses of action such as sending the young man or woman to a juvenile justice connection project for further analysis. There the offender may be referred to a psychiatrist, a counselor, or a medical doctor.

Often the recommendation is to refer the young person to a Back in Control Institute. This is done when the parents have lost control of their child. Parenting classes also are available at such institutes.

Juveniles who have been arrested have options:

- To be counseled and released.
  (The arrest remains, but it is kept low-key.)
- To have a court hearing.
  (The judge may grant probation depending on interviews with parents, family friends, teachers, etc. If probation is not granted, the matter is turned over to the district attorney's office.)

First-time offenders usually are sent to juvenile hall for a period of one to three months. This is a type of reform school with classes. Very strict rules and regulations are enforced.

Second-time offenders are sent to juvenile camp, where they can be held until reaching the age of twenty-five. Life for juvenile offenders at hall or camp can be hard because of all the restrictions and rules. The philosophy of both facilities, however, is to help get the young person back on the right track, not to administer severe punishment.

17

A very young child who commits a serious crime is interviewed to determine if he or she knows right from wrong. The child receives psychological testing and evaluation. If the crime is very serious, especially if drugs are involved, the child may be sent to juvenile hall.

Officers working with juveniles must be dedicated to their job. They work long, irregular hours and become involved with many families who are facing serious problems. Some may want help with those problems; others may resist any kind of assistance.

Every officer has some exposure to juvenile work in the course of his or her career, but some officers specialize in working with young people, in trying to prevent them from involvement with crime or drugs. These officers need patience and an understanding of human nature. The cases can be difficult, but many agree that the end rewards are worth the pains it takes to get there.

SPECIAL PROGRAMS OFFICERS

Many police officers are involved in special programs that focus on helping America's young people. Some work with local boys' and girls' clubs to help keep kids off the streets. Others volunteer to be a part of the national Big Brothers/Big Sisters program. A great number of officers are working in a drug prevention program called DARE: Drug Abuse Resistance Education.

Drug Abuse Resistance Education

DARE was developed in 1983 by the Los Angeles Police Department and the Los Angeles Unified School District; it now is being taught in more then 3,500 cities in 50 states.

DARE is a joint effort of local police departments and school districts. The program is taught by specially trained police officers to fifth- and sixth-grade students across the nation. DARE is aimed primarily at children who have not yet had a drug experience.

The DARE curriculum focuses on concepts of peer pressure resistance training, self-concept improvement, personal safety, and values decisions concerning respect for the law. The DARE instructors give students information and skills needed to resist peer pressure and to say no to alcohol and drugs. They try to improve the students' attitudes about themselves and to help them develop effective decision-making skills.

The program comprises seventeen weekly lessons at the elementary school level and nine lessons at the junior high/middle school level. Lessons focus on four major areas:

- Providing accurate information about tobacco, alcohol, and drugs
- Teaching students decision-making skills
- Showing students how to resist peer pressure
- Giving students ideas for alternatives to drug use.

DARE Lessons

A wide range of teaching activities are used in the program. Students take part in question-and-answer sessions, group discussions, role-playing activities, and workbook exercises. All activities are designed to encourage participation and response. The following are the first seventeen lessons:

- Practices for Personal Safety
  The DARE officer reviews common safety practices to protect students from harm at home, going to and from school, and in their neighborhood.
- Drug Use and Misuse
  Students learn the harmful effects of drug use

and view the film Drugs and Your Amazing Mind.

- Consequences
  The focus is on the consequences of using and not using alcohol and marijuana. Program instructors believe that by knowing the consequences of drug abuse, students can make better decisions regarding their own behavior.
- Resisting Pressure to Use Drugs
  The DARE officer explains different types of pressure—ranging from friendly persuasion to subtle teasing to outright threats—that friends, acquaintances, and others can exert on students to try tobacco, alcohol, or drugs.
- Resistance Techniques
  Students rehearse the many ways of refusing offers to try tobacco, alcohol, or drugs: simply saying no and repeating it as often as necessary; changing the subject; walking away; ignoring the person offering the drugs. Students learn that they can avoid situations in which they might be subjected to such pressures, and that it is helpful to hang around with nonusers.
- Building Self-Esteem
  Poor self-esteem is one of the factors associated with drug abuse. Young people who have little confidence and a low self-image are more likely to experiment with drugs and alcohol to make them feel better about themselves. In this session students learn to recognize their own positive qualities and how to compliment other people sincerely.
- Assertiveness: A Response Style
  Students have certain rights: to be themselves, to say what they think, to say no to offers of drugs. The session teaches them to assert those rights

confidently but without interfering with others' rights.

- Managing Stress Without Taking Drugs
Students learn to recognize sources of stress in their lives and learn techniques for avoiding or relieving stress. Some of these techniques are exercise, deep breathing, relaxation, and talking to others. Students learn that using drugs or alcohol to relieve stress can cause new problems and new stresses in their lives.
- Media Influences on Drug Use
The DARE officer reviews strategies used in the media to encourage tobacco and alcohol use, including testimonials from celebrities and social pressure.
- Decision-Making and Risk-Taking
Students learn the difference between bad risks and responsible risks, how to recognize the choices available to them, how to make a decision that promotes their own self-interest.
- Alternatives to Drug Abuse
Students learn that to have fun, to be accepted by peers, or to deal with feelings of anger or hurt, they have a number of alternatives to using drugs and alcohol.
- Role-Modeling
A high school student selected by the DARE officer visits the class, providing students with a positive role model. Students learn that drug users are in the minority.
- Forming a Support System
Students learn that they need to develop positive relationships with many different people and to form a support system.
- Ways to Deal with Pressures from Gangs
Students discuss the kinds of pressure they may

encounter from gang members and evaluate the consequences of the choices available to them.

- Project DARE Summary
Students summarize and assess what they have learned.
- Taking a Stand
Students compose and read aloud essays on how they can respond when they are pressured to use drugs and alcohol. The essay represents each student's "DARE pledge."
- Culmination
In a schoolwide assembly planned in concert with school administrators, all students who have participated in Project DARE receive certificates of achievement.

DARE instructors do not bombard students with scare tactics about the dangers of drug use. Instead, they work with the children to raise their self-esteem, to teach them to make decisions on their own, and to help them identify positive alternatives to tobacco, alcohol, and drug use.

DARE Officers

Officers who volunteer for the DARE program do so on the basis of a solid commitment to preventing substance abuse among young people. The officers must have clean records and a minimum of two years' experience patrolling the streets. They must be mature, communicate effectively, and be well organized.

The officers work in the community where they plan to participate. The exception is when communities are quite small or do not have resources to assign a local officer. In these communities, state police or sheriff's deputies can teach the program.

The selection process involves a preliminary screening of applicants and a formal interview by a review panel. The panel may include both police and school personnel. During these interviews, DARE candidates frequently reveal skills and experience that qualify them for this unique challenge in working with young people.

Training for DARE officers consists of a two-week, 80-hour seminar that is jointly presented by law-enforcement and education agencies. Several states now offer DARE officer training, which covers a number of areas:

- Current drug use patterns
- Prevention activities
- Communication and public speaking skills
- Classroom behavior
- School-police relationships
- Police-parent-community relationships
- Stages of adolescent chemical dependency
- Audiovisual skills
- Program administration
- Sources of supplementary funding

Each trainee prepares and teaches one lesson to fellow trainees, who play the roles of fifth- and sixth-graders. The trainee "instructor" is then evaluated by his or her "students" and offered suggestions for improving their performance.

One full-time law-enforcement officer is assigned for every ten elementary schools. The cost of the program is covered in part by the law-enforcement agency. Additional funds come from the Drug Free Schools and Communities Act of 1986, city funds, corporate donations, and private grants.

STARTING OUT AS A COP

Minimum Requirements

Age. To become a police officer, you must be at least 21 years old at the time you are hired and not yet 35 years old at the time you are interviewed. The age maximum of 35 years is provided by federal law.

Education. You must be a high school graduate or have a GED equivalent. Candidates who possess a GED must meet the current minimum requirements for a High School Equivalency Certificate in most states.

Citizenship. U.S. citizenship is not required prior to employment as a police officer. Noncitizens, however, must have applied for citizenship one year before applying to work as a police officer. Proof of citizenship or an application for citizenship is required during the selection process.

Vision. Vision must be correctable to at least 20/30 by either glasses or contact lenses, with the following restrictions:

- Eyeglasses or hard contact lenses—uncorrected distance visual acuity of at least 20/70 in the poorer eye and 20/40 in the other.
- Soft contact lenses—no limit on uncorrected distance visual acuity, provided soft lenses have been worn for at least 1 year prior to the physical examination. Normal color vision is required.

Health. Police academies give recruits eight weeks to nine months of intense training. You must be in excellent health, with no conditions that would restrict

24

your ability to complete academy training or to perform police work.

Qualifications

To become a police officer a candidate goes through a basic selection process. Today's selection process is much shorter than in the past, where an applicant had to wait six to eight months for an answer. Successful candidates can expect to enter the police academy within a few months. The selection process consists of the following steps:

- Written test
- Interview
- Medical examination
- Written psychological test battery
- Physical abilities test
- Background investigation
- Psychological evaluation

A candidate must complete the steps of the selection process in order. The Personnel Department is responsible to the Board of Civil Service Commissioners for administering all tests.

Written Test. A 45-minute, multiple-choice test, it is designed to measure reading comprehension, English usage (including spelling and vocabulary), reasoning, and the ability to make common-sense judgments on practical problems.

Interview. Candidates who pass the written test usually are interviewed soon thereafter. The interview lasts about 30 minutes. The interviewer is a sworn member of the police department, usually a supervising sergeant or a departmental detective. Questions focus on the

25

candidate's work experience, education, ability to relate well to others, ability to reason and solve problems, and communications skills.

Medical Examination and Written Psychological Test. All candidates who pass the interview with a referable score (which varies according to hiring needs) are scheduled for a medical exam and a written psychological test. Both are given on the same day at the same place and require about five or six hours to complete.

The medical examination is administered by a doctor employed by the Occupational Health and Safety Division of the Personnel Department. It is a thorough examination. Therefore, it is essential that candidates be in excellent health and have body fat content appropriate for their height and weight.

The written psychological test consists of three parts: the Minnesota Multiphasic Personality Inventory, the Sixteen Personality Factor Inventory, and a personal history questionnaire. The test results are evaluated by staff psychologists.

Background Investigation. Next, candidates are scheduled for fingerprints, photographs, and background interviews. These take place on the same day. The background check is made through police records, personal and employment histories, and field reference checks. Candidates are evaluated as to respect for the law, honesty, mature judgment, respect for others, and honorable military record. All candidates submit comprehensive biographical information prior to their background interview.

Physical Abilities Test. Candidates who successfully complete the medical examination are scheduled for the physical abilities test (PAT), designed to measure physical endurance, strength, and agility. The test varies from state to state but typically includes the following items:

- *Endurance Run*
  Run as many laps as possible in 12 minutes on a 1/8 mile track.
- *Wall Scale*
  Run 50 yards, then scale a smooth wall six feet high.
- *Maintain Grip*
  Run 5 yards, then take an overhand grip on the chinning bar. Maintain the grip while hanging free for one minute.
- *Weight Drag*
  Run 50 feet, then drag a deadweight of 140 pounds for 50 feet.

Psychological Interview. Candidates are scheduled for this interview if it appears that they will be successful in their background investigation. Candidates are interviewed by a city psychologist and evaluated for judgment, emotional stability, and real interest in the job.

When a candidate has successfully completed all formal examinations, he or she is placed on an eligibility list. After being appointed and completing a probationary period, the candidate becomes a permanent employee of the police agency.

TRAINING FOR POLICE WORK

Training for a career in law enforcement can begin as early as the moment you decide to enter the field. You can begin by taking high school courses in law, civics, history, and psychology. You should also learn typing and computer skills. Knowledge of a foreign language can prove helpful if you work in a region that has a high ethnic concentration.

Basic Training

Basic police training programs vary widely in length and content, depending on the size of the force. Smaller police agencies usually provide more on-the-job training. Larger agencies tend to focus on formal instruction that lasts from several weeks to six months. Typical subjects might include the following:

- Criminal law
- Motor vehicle codes
- Arrest procedures
- Methods of surveillance
- Accident investigation
- Laws of evidence
- Crowd control
- First aid
- Armed or unarmed defense techniques

Police officers must be prepared to deal with a variety of emergencies both day and night. Much of the work revolves around problems with people, such as squabbles between husband and wife or landlord and tenant. Police must be able to handle these problems in addition to cases of child abuse, multicar crashes with injuries, or burglary or vandalism. This is why the training covers such a variety of subjects, from rules and regulations to psychology. Recruits must know how to defend both themselves and others.

Laser Training

One important area of training for recruits is the proper care and use of firearms. Training courses have made great advances in the teaching of firearms use. A newly developed laser training course shows dramatically what happens when an officer comes face to face with a potential killer.

The tools used are a laser transmitter, an electronic vest, and a shotgun converted to fire a laser beam. The laser unit and its 7-volt battery fit into the gun barrel. The beam that it shoots has a range of about 66 feet. The vest has three full-length panels on front and back. About six inches from the top of each panel is a grommet that contains a light bulb. If the laser beam hits any part of that panel, the light begins to blink and a sound is heard warning the wearer that he or she has been hit.

The officer in training puts on the vest and takes a loaded laser gun. He or she is told that a suspect (another laser vest hung on a rack) is somewhere in the building. When the officer finds the target, he or she draws and fires, scoring hits on the vest. If the officer is hit, his or her vest lights flash on and the warning sound is heard.

While the scene is in progress, the action is watched by a training officer who is a certified firearms instructor. The test shows whether the officer-in-training drew and fired or froze in panic. The situations are very realistic; a candidate who fails the first encounter and ends up shot often is badly shaken from the experience.

Beyond Basic Training

When a rookie graduates from basic training, he or she should have the general skills needed for serving on regular assignments. The officer remains under the guidance of another officer, and in some departments the rookie may continue taking classes on a variety of subjects.

After an officer has worked in the field, he or she may wish to enter a more specialized area of police work, such as criminal investigation or vice. The department provides specialized training in other areas of police work, and courses also are given at a number of colleges and at a variety of agencies, such as the Federal Bureau of Investigation.

OPPORTUNITIES FOR WOMEN AND MINORITIES

Female police officers have been employed throughout the country for a number of decades. Until the early 1970s, however, their work consisted of writing parking tickets and handling paperwork. A few female officers were assigned to work with female juvenile offenders.

This led to litigation and legislation, and today women are no longer subject to different hiring practices or inferior wages or job assignments. By the mid-1970s, female officers' roles had been expanded to include street patrols, and now women account for a significant and steadily growing number of officers in the nation.

Some prejudices still remain, however. An order by a female officer may be challenged by a criminal who thinks the officer is less qualified physically and emotionally. Female officers may have a tougher time getting their point across.

In an effort to encourage female recruits, a number of police departments offer the Crime Prevention Assistant (CPA) program to qualified officer candidates waiting to begin recruit training. Although the program is open to any minority candidate with a need for assistance, it is targeted to help females with their academic and physical training needs.

The program offers candidates an opportunity to strengthen their areas of weakness before entering the police academy. They are paid during training. Candidates who participate have a lower dropout rate than those who have not taken the course.

The eight-week program consists of extensive physical and psychological preparatory training, instruction in a variety of academic subject areas, and tips on equipment care and use. CPAs are required to meet and maintain minimum standards in physical training, academics, and general character.

Law enforcement agencies today offer employment to all minorities. The requirement is that all candidates must successfully complete all steps in the selection process.

SALARIES

Police salaries are dependent upon individual qualifications, experience, and education; the type and function of employing agency; and area of the country. An officer's pay is of two types: base pay and extra pay. Base pay is the established salary as determined by rank, length of time in rank, and length of service. Extra pay is money paid in addition to usual compensation.

The average entry-level salary ranges between $23,000 and $30,000. Most agencies offer substantial benefit packages that include life and medical insurance, paid vacations, pension plans, clothing allowances, and pay increases. An officer who is injured on the job can expect to receive medical care and expenses and continued pay during the recuperation period.

Many benefits cover the officer and his or her family as well. The following is an example of a police officer's benefit package. Figures, dates, and time vary from state to state.

Holidays:	13 paid holidays a year.
Days Off:	8 days off during every 28-day deployment period.
Paid Vacations:	15 calendar days per year during the first 10 years of service; 22 days per year after 10 years of service.
Sick	12 days per calendar year at full pay; 5

Leave: days per year at 75 percent pay; 5 days per year at 50 percent pay.

Family Illness Leave: 5 days per calendar year at full pay of unused sick leave for illness in the immediate family.

Bereavement Leave: 3 days at full pay for death in the immediate family.

Health Insurance: The city pays $301 per month maximum for approved health plans covering employees and their dependents. This contribution will be increased as health plan costs rise.

Dental Insurance: The city pays $27 per month maximum for approved dental plans covering employees and their dependents. This contribution will be increased as dental plan costs rise.

Life Insurance: The city pays $12 per month toward the cost of the Police Protective League-sponsored life insurance plan. This contribution will rise as costs of the plan rise.

Uniform Allowance: $600 per year to cover the costs of uniform maintenance and replacement.

Bonus Pay: Additional compensation may be provided for marksmanship skills, bilingual ability, longevity, and hazardous duty.

Education: Several scholarships and professional training programs are available to officers who wish to continue their education. In addition, the city reimburses tuition for approved degree programs at rates equivalent to current university fees.

Pensions: Upon completion of academy training, all officers become members of the police department pension fund. Eight percent is deducted from regular pay. A minimum of 10 years of service is required to qualify for retirement benefits; retired officers must be at least 50 years of age to receive benefits. The amount received is based on years of service and the officer's final average salary.

JOB OUTLOOK
Through the year 2000, jobs for police are expected to increase as fast as jobs in the overall economy. Demand continues to grow in large cities where the supply of qualified people can be limited.

Employment growth, however, may be limited by budget restraints at the federal and state levels. Turnover rate for police is among the lowest of all occupations, and most job openings will be to replace workers who retire, transfer to other occupations, or stop working for other reasons.

COLLEGES AND UNIVERSITIES OFFERING COURSES AND/OR DEGRESS IN LAW ENFORCEMENT AND POLICE SCIENCE
A—Associate degree
B—Bachelor's degree
M—Master's degree
D—Doctorate
C—Certificate
X—Executive

Law Enforcement
Alabama
Gadsden State Community College, A
Jacksonville State University, BM
Jefferson State Community College, A
Lurleen B. Wallace State Junior College, A
Marion Military Institute, A
Northwest Alabama State Community College, A
Samford University, B

Alaska
Sheldon Jackson College, A
University of Alaska Southeast—Sitka Campus, C

Arizona
Eastern Arizona College, A
Mesa Community College, A
Phoenix College, A

Arkansas
University of Arkansas—Little Rock, A

California
Bakersfield College, A
Cabrillo College, CA
College of the Redwoods, A
College of the Sequoias, CA
De Anza College, CA
Modesto Junior College, A
Mount San Antonio College, A
Ohlone College, A
Sierra College, A
Solano Community College, CA
Southwestern College, CA

Colorado
Trinidad State Junior College, A

Connecticut
Manchester Community Technical College, CA
Middlesex Community Technical College, A
University of Hartford, B
University of New Haven, B
Western Connecticut State University, B

Delaware
Wilmington College, B

Florida
Broward Community College, A

Florida Atlantic University, B
Palm Beach Community College, A
Polk Community College, CA
Saint Petersburg Junior College, A
Santa Fe Community College, A
Tallahassee Community College, A

Georgia
Andrew College, A

Idaho
College of Southern Idaho, CA
Lewis-Clark State College, AB
North Idaho College, CA
Ricks College, A

Illinois
Belleville Area College, CA
Carl Sandburg College, CA
City Colleges of Chicago—Harry S. Truman College,
  CA
City Colleges of Chicago—Richard J. Daley College,
  CA
John Wood Community College, CA
Joliet Junior College, CA
Kankakee Community College, CA
Kishwaukee College, CA
Lake Land College, CA
Lincoln College, A
Morton College, A
Oakton Community College, A
Southeastern Illinois College, CA
Southern Illinois University at Carbondale, A

Indiana
University of Indianapolis, AB

Iowa
Clinton Community College, A

Des Moines Area Community College—Boone Campus, A
Iowa Central Community College—Eagle Grove Center, A
Iowa Central Community College—Fort Dodge Center, A
Iowa Lakes Community College—Emmetsburg Campus, A
Iowa Western Community College—Clarinda Campus, A
Kirkwood Community College, A
North Iowa Area Community College, A

Kansas
Kansas City Kansas Community College, A
Seward County Community College, CA

Kentucky
Murray State University, AB
Northern Kentucky University, A

Louisiana
Grambling State University, AB
Louisiana State University—Eunice, A
Southern University and Agricultural and Mechanical College, A

Maryland
Anne Arundel Community College, CA
Chesapeake College, CA
Hagerstown Junior College, A
New Community College of Baltimore, A
University of Baltimore, CB
University of Maryland—College Park Campus, B

Massachusetts
Dean Junior College, A
Holyoke Community College, A

Massasoit Community College, A
Northeastern University, AB
Western New England College, B

Michigan
Alpena Community College, A
Glen Oaks Community College, CA
Henry Ford Community College, A
Jackson Community College, CA
Kalamazoo Valley Community College, A
Kellogg Community College, A
Kirtland Community College, A
Lake Michigan College, A
Lake Superior State University, AB
Macomb Community College, CA
Monroe County Community College, A
Northwestern Michigan College, A
Oakland Community College—Auburn Hills Campus,
   CA
Oakland Community College—Orchard Ridge Campus,
   A
Oakland Community College—Royal Oak Campus, A
Schoolcraft College, A
Washtenaw Community College, C
West Shore Community College, A

Minnesota
Hibbing Community College, A
Lakewood State Community College, A
Mesabi Community College, A
Metropolitan State University, B
Minneapolis Community College, A
Normandale Community College, A
North Hennepin Community College, A
Northland Community College, A
Rochester Community College, A
Willmar Community College, A

Mississippi
Jones County Junior College, A
Northeast Mississippi Community College, A
Southwest Mississippi Junior College, A

Missouri
Jefferson College, CA
Missouri Southern State College, A
Three Rivers Community College, CA

Montana
Dawson Community College, A

Nebraska
Metropolitan Community College, A

Nevada
Truckee Meadows Community College, A

New Jersey
Cumberland County College, CA
Gloucester County College, A
Mercer County Community College, A
Thomas Edison State College, AB

New Mexico
New Mexico Junior College, A

North Carolina
Alamance Community College, A
College of The Albemarle, C
Isothermal Community College, A
Pfeiffer College, B
Rockingham Community College, A
Rowan Technical College, A
Southwestern Community College, A
Surry Community College, A
Wayne Community College, A
Western Carolina University, B
Wilson Technical Community College, A

North Dakota
Minot State University, BM

Ohio
Cuyahoga Community College—District, A
Cuyahoga Community College—Eastern Campus, A
Jefferson Technical College, A
Muskingum Area Technical Institute, A
Sinclair Community College, A
Terra Technical College, A
Tiffin University, AB
University of Toledo, A

Oklahoma
Connors State College, A
East Central University, B
Northeastern Oklahoma Agricultural and Mechanical
  Junior College, CA
Northern Oklahoma College, A
Northwestern Oklahoma State University, B
Oklahoma City University, B
Oklahoma Panhandle State University, A
Western Oklahoma State College, A

Oregon
Lane Community College, A
Treasure Valley Community College, A
Western Oregon State College, B

Pennsylvania
Community College of Beaver County, A
Lehigh County Community College, C
Reading Area Community College, A

Puerto Rico
Inter American University of Puerto Rico, A

Rhode Island
Community College of Rhode Island—Knight Campus,
  A

South Carolina
University of South Carolina, M

Tennessee
Middle Tennessee State University, A

Texas
Bee County College, A
Blinn College, CA
Central Texas College, CA
Cisco Junior College, A
Cooke County College, A
Dallas Baptist University, B
East Texas State University, B
Grayson County College, A
Howard College, A
Laredo Junior College, A
McLennan Community College, CA
Navarro College, A
Odessa College, A
Paris Junior College, CA
Prairie View A&M University, B
Sam Houston State University, B
San Jacinto College—Central Campus, CA
San Jacinto College—North Campus, CA
Southwest Texas State University, B
University of Mary Hardin—Baylor, B
Wharton County Junior College, A

Vermont
Champlain College, A

Virginia
George Mason University, B
Old Dominion University, A

Washington
Bellevue Community College, A

Green River Community College, A
Lower Columbia College, A
Spokane Community College, A

West Virginia
Bluefield State College, A

Wisconsin
Silver Lake College, B

Alberta
Grant MacEwan Community College, X

Law Enforcement & Corrections
Alabama
Troy State University in Montgomery, ABM

California
San Bernardino Valley College, CA

Georgia
Atlanta Metropolitan College, A

Indiana
Vincennes University, A

Maryland
Cecil Community College, CA

North Carolina
University of North Carolina—Wilmington, B

Ohio
Cuyahoga Community College—Western Campus, A
Lakeland Community College, A

Oklahoma
Oklahoma State University—Oklahoma City, A

Texas
Midland College, A

41

Virginia
Averett College, B
Mountain Empire Community College, A

Law Enforcement & Criminology
Maryland
University of Maryland—University College, CAB

Massachusetts
Springfield Technical Community College, A

Law Enforcement Administration
Illinois
Lincoln Land Community College, CA
Western Illinois University, BM

Michigan
Wayne County Community College, CA

New Jersey
Camden County College, A

Oklahoma
University of Oklahoma, B

Texas
Alvin Community College, CA

Law Enforcement Technology

Florida
Daytona Beach Community College, C

Georgia
Atlanta Metropolitan College, A

Illinois
Black Hawk College—Quad Cities Campus, A

Kentucky
Hopkinsville Community College, A

University of Kentucky—Community College System, A

Maine
Southern Maine Technical College, A

North Carolina
Asheville-Buncombe Technical Community College, A
Beaufort County Community College, A
Bladen Community College, A
Guilford Technical Community College, A
Halifax Community College, A
Randolph Community College, C

Ohio
Columbus State Community College, CA
Lima Technical College, A
Owens Technical College, A

Texas
Temple Junior College, A

Police Administration
California
Bakersfield College, CA

Florida
Lake-Sumter Community College, A

Kentucky
Eastern Kentucky University, AB

Michigan
Henry Ford Community College, A

Pennsylvania
Bucks County Community College, CA
Harrisburg Area Community College, A

Police Science

Alabama
John C. Calhoun State Community College, A

California
Citrus College, A
College of San Mateo, CA
College of the Redwoods, A
College of the Sequoias, CA
Compton Community College, A
Diablo Valley College, CA
El Camino College, CA
Fresno City College, CA
Fullerton College, CA
Gavilan College, CA
Glendale Community College, CA
Imperial Valley College, CA
Los Angeles Harbor College, A
Los Angeles Valley College, A
Marin Community College, A
Merced College, CA
Merritt College, A
Modesto Junior College, A
Mount San Jacinto College, CA
Pasadena City College, A
Rio Hondo College, CA
Saddleback College, A
San Joaquin Delta College, CA
Santa Monica College, CA
Santa Rosa Junior College, CA
Southwestern College, CA
Victor Valley College, CA
West Hills Community College, A

Florida
Broward Community College, CA

Georgia
DeKalb Technical Institute, A

Illinois
Illinois Central College, A
Prairie State College, CA
Rock Valley College, CA

Iowa
Hawkeye Community College, A
Western Iowa Tech Community College, A

Kansas
Colby Community College, A
Cowley County Community College, CA
Garden City Community College, A
Labette Community College, A

Kentucky
University of Louisville, CABM

Michigan
Muskegon Community College, A
North Central Michigan College, A
Oakland Community College—Orchard Ridge Campus, A
Oakland Community College—Royal Oak Campus, A

Mississippi
Hinds Community College, A

Missouri
Longview Community College, A
Penn Valley Community College, A
Three Rivers Community College, A

New Jersey
Middlesex County College, A

New Mexico
New Mexico State University—Las Cruces, AB
University of New Mexico—Gallup Branch, C

New York
John Jay College of Criminal Justice of the City University of New York, AB
State University of New York, Adirondack Community College, A
State University of New York, Community College of the Finger Lakes, A
State University of New York, Monroe Community College, A
State University of New York, Nassau Community College, A
State University of New York, Orange County Community College, A
State University of New York, Suffolk County Community College, A

North Carolina
Coastal Carolina Community College, A
Durham Technical Community College, A
Fayetteville State University, AB
Forsyth Technical Community College, A
Pitt Community College, A
Robeson Technical College, A
Western Piedmont Community College, A

Ohio
Hocking Technical College, CA
Lorain County Community College, CA
Youngstown State University, CA

Oklahoma
Rogers State College, A

Pennsylvania
Community College of Allegheny County, Boyce
   Campus, A
Community College of Beaver County, CA
Harrisburg Area Community College, CA
Montgomery County Community College, A

Puerto Rico
Caribbean University, B
University of Puerto Rico—Carolina Regional College,
   A

Tennessee
Roane State Community College, A
Walters State Community College, C

Texas
Del Mar College, A
Lee College, A
University of Central Texas, B

Utah
Southern Utah University, CA
Weber State University, AB

Virginia
Danville Community College, A
John Tyler Community College, CA
New River Community College, A
Northern Virginia Community College, CA
Piedmont Virginia Community College, A
Southside Virginia Community College, CA
Thomas Nelson Community College, A
Virginia Highlands Community College, A
Wytheville Community College, CA

Washington
Skagit Valley College, A

West Virginia
Marshall University, A

Wisconsin
Blackhawk Technical College, A
Chippewa Valley Technical College, A
Fox Valley Technical Institute, A
Gateway Technical College, A
Lakeshore Technical College, A
Madison Area Technical College, A
Mid-State Technical Institute, A
Milwaukee Area Technical College, A
Nicolet Area Technical College, A
North Central Technical Institute, A
Northeast Wisconsin Technical College, A
Waukesha County Technical Institute, A
Western Wisconsin Technical College, A

Wyoming
Sheridan College, A

U.S. Territories
University of the Virgin Islands, A

From *The College Blue Book* (New York: Macmillan), 1993.

3

Careers in Sheriff and U.S. Marshal Work

Men and women employed as sheriffs and deputy sheriffs usually enforce the law in rural areas or places where there is no local police department. Sheriffs keep the peace in various areas of a county or city, including areas with mountainous terrain, dense forests, and water.

Sheriffs are authorized to make arrests, and they may execute a variety of court orders, such as summoning jurors and distributing money or property judgments. They may guard prisoners or oversee trials. Many work with transportation bureaus, helping to maintain buses that carry prisoners to and from court. Sheriffs also guard against escapes and keep incoming prisoners under control.

If a witness is scheduled to testify at a trial, he or she may be notified by a sheriff. The sheriff can go to a witness' place of business or home to serve court papers requiring appearance. A sheriff also acts as the courtroom bailiff, bringing in prisoners to appear before the judge and handing documents and evidence from the attorneys to the judge overseeing the courtroom.

Sheriffs also perform essential police functions. They preserve the peace, investigate crime, enforce traffic regulations, and participate in search and rescue operations.

Jobs available in a sheriff's department vary from state to state. Most positions, however, fall in the following areas:

- Administrative
- Court services
- Custody
- Technical Services
- Detective

A number of sheriff's department employees are members of special teams that focus on specific areas of law enforcement. Some special teams are the following:

- Aero Bureau
- Background Investigation
- Canine Unit
- Court Services
- Detective Units (homicide, narcotics, vice, and juvenile)
- Marine Patrol
- Mounted Enforcement (horseback)
- Search and Rescue
- Special Weapons Team

Search and Rescue Teams

Sheriffs departments are using state-of-the-art crime fighting and rescue equipment to do their jobs more effectively. One area that stands out with its heavy use of this equipment is the search and rescue group called the Law Enforcement Aerial Patrol, or LEAP.

LEAP is a group of airborne helicopter rescuers who are called upon when air power is the only way to respond to a disaster. LEAP members perform rescue operations during torrential rains, flooding, and earthquakes when it may be impossible for rescue workers on land to reach those in need of help.

Sometimes LEAP members must go to hazardous mountain areas where fire, wind, smoke, and jagged treetops make it difficult for a helicopter to land. Because of this, a technique called rope rescue has been developed.

During a rope rescue, a LEAP member jumps out of an aircraft on a fixed rope. Two 6,000-pound-test dacron lines are attached to a harness and secured to the helicopter floor. A litter is dropped to a waiting ground team. Speed is essential during these rescue operations; often there is no second chance to retrieve an accident victim.

One ground-team rescue worker clips his or her harness to the line strung from the helicopter to the ground team. The rescue worker and the injured party are both lifted out of the hazardous area. This process, called extraction, is directed by the helicopter crew chief.

Crew chiefs require intensive training and must be able to handle high-stress situations in tight quarters. Recruits may start out on patrol with an experienced observer. After 2,000 hours of patrol experience, they receive training in desert rescue, and finally, in mountain rescue. Most rescue fliers have at least five years of police experience, and most fly an average of 1,000 hours per year.

Job Requirements

Requirements to become a sheriff vary from state to state, but usually the applicant must:

- Be at least 20 1/2 years old at time of filing.
- Be a U.S. citizen.

51

- Have a valid driver's license.
- Be a high school graduate or have the GED equivalent.
- Be in good physical condition.
- Be of good moral character.

Applicants also are required to pass a written and an oral examination. The written exam evaluates reading comprehension and writing skills.

The oral interview takes only a few minutes. It is simply an exchange of information, and the grade is pass or fail. The applicant talks about him or herself and shows his or her knowledge of the department and understanding of the duties of a sheriff. The interviewer evaluates applicants based on their initial impression, their interest in the position, their appearance and attire, and their communication skills.

In addition to the written and oral exams, applicants must demonstrate ability to complete a job-related work sample test battery, such as running a 99-yard obstacle course and climbing a solid and a chain-link fence.

Finally, a thorough background investigation is performed, including a fingerprint search and polygraph (lie detector) examination. Candidates can be disqualified for any felony conviction, job-related misdemeanor conviction, serious traffic conviction, poor credit history, poor employment history, substance abuse (alcohol or drugs), or driving under the influence of alcohol.

Training
Cadets are trained in all aspects of law enforcement. The curriculum includes patrol procedures, criminal law, juvenile procedures, traffic criminal investigations, defense tactics, driver's training, and the use and care of firearms. After passing tests on academic and physical ability, cadets graduate as deputy sheriffs.

Benefits

Benefit packages vary from state to state, but they generally include paid holidays, sick leave, promotional opportunities, military leave, health and insurance plans, vacations, and retirement plans.

Related Job Opportunities

The following are related job opportunities:

Beach patrol	Legal deputy
Driver training instructor	Narcotics agent
Fire safety	Polygraph examiner
Firearms examiner	Process server
Forensic and voice I.D.	Traffic enforcer
Helicopter pilot	Homicide investigator
Vice investigator	Juvenile investigator
Weapons Training Instructor	

WORKING IN THE U.S. MARSHALS SERVICE

The U.S. Marshals Service, established in 1789, is the oldest federal law-enforcement agency. It is a bureau of the Department of Justice and includes 93 Presidentially appointed U.S. Marshals and about 2,700 civil servants throughout the United States, Puerto Rico, the Virgin Islands, Guam, and the Northern Mariana Islands.

Job Responsibilities

Employees of the U.S. Marshals Service provide protection to the federal courts, judges, jurors, and witnesses. Others apprehend federal fugitives, transport federal prisoners, or execute court orders.

The Service handles the custody, management, and sale of property that is seized from criminals, and it administers the National Asset Seizure and Forfeiture

53

Program. The Service also manages the operation of the Witness Security Program.

Job Qualifications

Most entry-level jobs in the Marshals Service are for Deputy U.S. Marshals. Applicants for these positions must take a written test. Most applicants have earned bachelor's degrees. Although the Service considers applicants with majors in almost any field, it specifically looks for people with degrees in accounting, budgeting, business administration, computer science, criminal justice, criminology, data processing, economics, personnel administration, police administration, police science, and public administration.

For additional information, visit your local library or write the U.S. Marshals Service, 600 Army-Navy Drive, Arlington, VA 22202.

4.

Careers as Detectives and Criminologists

Detectives are plain-clothes investigators who gather facts and collect evidence in criminal cases. They conduct interviews, examine records, observe the activities of suspects, and participate in raids or arrests. Most detectives are assigned to the criminal investigations division after several years on patrol duty.

In large police departments, detectives are organized into specialized units such as the homicide division, the narcotics division, or the arson division. Other units include gambling, prostitution, and robbery.

Detectives do some of their work at a desk and some out in the field. They usually start their investigation of a crime with the initial crime report of the responding police officer(s).

Detectives gather difficult-to-obtain information. They receive help in their investigations from forensic specialists, or criminologists. These specialists are trained to examine the scene of a crime, the victims, and any crime-related vehicles for physical evidence.

Criminologists search crime scenes for fingerprints, broken locks, and broken glass. They look for blood, skin, or hair traces. They take photographs, make sketches, and make casts of footprints and tire tracks.

Criminologists also include handwriting experts, finger-print and voiceprint specialists, lie detector examiners, and tooth and bite-mark specialists.

Some physical evidence is tested by specially trained crime lab technicians. The results of these tests and information about the other evidence is given to the detective assigned to the case. The detective adds to this information by interviewing victims and witnesses, talking to informers, and conducting surveillance oper-ations. They also sift through existing police files on other crimes, on known criminals, and on people sus-pected of criminal activity, searching for links to their case. Throughout this research process, the detective writes detailed reports about his or her findings.

CRIMINAL INVESTIGATION TECHNIQUES

Interrogation
To investigate a crime, information has to be obtained. Just as a private investigator digs for facts to put a case together, so does the police detective in investigating a criminal case. The criminal investigator asks questions of people who have knowledge of the crime—a victim's neighbor or friend or family member. Suspects are interrogated. Eyewitnesses to a crime are asked to identify the perpetrator. Experiments under controlled conditions indicate that jurors convict four times as often if eyewitness testimony is offered.

Fingerprints
Another method of identification is fingerprinting. The lab experts use the impression made by the small ridge formations or patterns on the underside of the ends of the fingers.

You may have had your fingerprints taken for one reason or another. If you are applying for a business license or taking the bar exam, fingerprints are required. These imprints are put on file in an identification system. When an arrest is made, copies of the suspect's prints are sent to the state identification system and to the FBI in Washington, DC. If the suspect is wanted by a law enforcement agency, a notice in the file at the National Crime Information Center of the FBI alerts the interested agency of the status and location of the person.

No two persons have exactly the same arrangement of ridge patterns, and the pattern remains unchanged through life. Many police departments are now using facsimile machines to transmit fingerprints, photography, and other information from a central file. For example, a fiber found on a screen door at the scene of a burglary may be associated with a suspect's sweater, or a hair found on a suspect's truck in a hit-and-run may help prove that the truck struck the victim.

The laboratory of the FBI, the crime laboratory, and a number of cities employ criminologists. Investigations are conducted at municipal, state, and federal levels.

It is the job of the criminologists to identify evidence as to its nature and source. Fingerprints, shoe impressions, blood samples, hair follicles, and most recently DNA matching are some of the methods used to place a suspect at the scene of a crime. Great progress is being made in the matching of DNA patterns. A minute strand of hair, a flake of skin, or a drop of blood is now enough to match a person's DNA pattern with a sample of one left at the scene of a crime.

The crime labs have many names. They are called:

- Police labs
- Criminology labs
- Forensic science labs

Scientists in these labs require an understanding of law and criminal investigation and a familiarity with all aspects of criminal justice. They must be able to outthink and outguess the cleverest criminals.

Sometimes the scientists have nothing more to work with than a shred of clothing or a few pieces of bone in trying to determine the cause of death. They must use their knowledge and experience in trying to piece together what happened. The experts are grateful for new technologies that help them in their work. The spectrophotometer is an instrument that enables the criminologist to compare colors and classification of colors. He or she can identify and compare dyes, inks, paint, fibers, and other substances.

Recently, science has provided substantial aid to crime detection. High-power microscopes are used to see even the smallest piece of evidence. Computers and newly developed lab equipment assist experts in finding answers to unsolved cases. The single hair found on a murder victim can be brought to the lab and analyzed. A minute chip of paint found on the sweater of a hit-and-run victim can lead the police to the vehicle. Anything in the physical universe has the potential of becoming evidence in an investigation. Procedures used in analyzing and interpreting evidence include the examining of firearms, toxicological and serological tests, metallurgical tests, and document examinations.

Firearms Examination
How can a gun expert decide if a bullet came from a particular gun? He can assume it was used or believe eyewitness stories, but because of the seriousness of the crime he must be sure. The firearms expert can determine whether bullets match a gun by microscopic im-

perfections that are produced in gun barrels during manufacture.

Firing a gun leaves a mark or a "signature" on the bullet. When a bullet is fired, rough places inside the gun barrel leave certain marks on it. The grooves in the barrel also leave impressions on the bullet. Two bullets fired from the same gun have identical groove impressions and marks, which are matched for a positive or negative identification.

Other parts of the gun also have individual characteristics. The extractor and ejector and the breech face come in contact with the cartridge case, which may be scarred with distinctive markings. Use and wear of a firearm contribute further to the weapon's individuality.

Serological Investigations

Experts in the serological lab study body fluids. Often they are called upon to determine whether a bloodstain on a piece of clothing matches the blood of a victim or suspect. Serological procedures are applied to determine whether a bloodstain is human or animal in origin and its blood-group classification. A suspect in a murder with bloodstains found on his or her clothing may say that it is the blood of an animal. Certain lab tests can immediately identify the origin of the blood and its breakdown and composition.

Most people have A, B, O, or AB blood type. Another test separates Rh+ from Rh−. Each group is based on a particular chemical substance in the blood. Blood groups are inherited and never change.

Serological tests on dried bloodstains can ascertain whether the blood could have come from the suspect or the victim. These tests provide valuable evidence in prosecuting criminal cases.

Toxicology

Another type of lab that is used in criminal investigations is the toxicology lab, where poison samples are studied. Experts put the poisons through series of steps to get rid of all the substances that would be present normally.

The specimens ordinarily examined in cases of suspected poisoning are tissue samples from vital organs, blood or urine, food, drink, and the suspected poison itself.

When a person is found dead with no apparent cause, experts can determine through urine or blood samples if a poison is present and what that poison is.

Metallurgical Investigations

Metallurgical examinations make it possible to identify the manufacturer of a wire or a tool or other metallic material found at a crime scene. Using modern technological equipment, experts can trace the evidence to its owner.

Metallurgical examinations can be of great value in hit-and-run cases. Often some part of the vehicle is left behind, such as a piece of fender or a hubcap. Lab workers can trace these parts to the owners by finding out what make and model of car the fragments came from.

In many cases vehicles have been located by just a metal fragment found at the scene of the accident Examiners make a great contribution to the solution of crimes. The job requires attention to detail and ability to investigate even the smallest piece of information.

Document Examination

A blank check was stolen and written out for $1,000. The thief then forged the owner's name and cashed the check at a nearby bank. The victim knew who the forger was and told the police, who searched the suspect's apartment and found what looked like a matching signature. Before any conclusions could be made, both documents were submitted to the lab and experts began their work. They were able to identify the signature on the check as the same signature found in the suspect's home.

The lab can also identify typewriting, inks and paper, and writing left on charred paper by using various types of high-power microscopes.

Forensic experts also include voiceprint specialists, lie detector examiners, and odontologists (tooth and bite-mark specialists).

Narcotics Lab

Police officers and chemists are employed as experts in the narcotics lab. Their backgrounds include police training and college degrees in chemistry. Many who work in this field can recognize certain drugs by sight.

In examining marijuana, for example, the lab scientist may recognize it as such but perform certain lab tests to confirm the identification. The scientist weighs the drug, examines it under a microscope, and performs color tests to confirm the conclusion.

Other chemical methods are used to identify heroin. The substance is measured, filtered, mixed, and dissolved to find out exactly what drug is present and in what amount.

JOB REQUIREMENTS

Students interested in detective work should take a diverse course load that includes English, American history, business law, government, psychology, sociology, chemistry, and physics, as well as courses in journalism and a foreign language. Classes in computer use and typing are necessary.

To become a police detective, you must first gain experience as a police officer. After about three to five years on a police force, officers may be promoted to detective. In some departments, candidates must pass a written examination and participate in a training program. The programs vary in length from a few weeks to several months.

Students interested in jobs as criminologists should focus on acquiring skills in the specialty field in which they want to work. A degree in chemistry, biology, electronics, or whatever field is appropriate should be obtained.

In addition to a specialized degree, prospective criminologists should take classes in forensic science. These are offered by some colleges and by law-enforcement training programs and police departments.

EARNINGS

Salaries for police detectives range from about $18,900 to $37,300 a year. As a detective gains more experience, his or her salary increases considerably. Benefits include health insurance, paid vacation, sick days, and pension plans.

Crime lab personnel earn between $13,000 and $20,000 annually. Many specialists, however, have higher earnings.

Employment Outlook

The employment outlook for both detectives and criminologists is expected to be average into the 21st century. Most of the openings will result from employees retiring or leaving their department for other reasons.

Additional Sources of Information

American Federation of Police
3801 Biscayne Boulevard
Miami, FL 33137

American Society of Criminology
1314 Kinnear Road
Columbus, OH 43212

DEA Headquarters
1405 I Street NW
Washington, DC 20537

Federal Bureau of Investigation
Applicant Coordinator
10th and Pennsylvania Avenue, NW
Washington, DC 20520

International Association of Chiefs of Police
515 North Washington Street
Alexandria, VA 22314

5

The FBI and CIA

The Federal Bureau of Investigation is the primary investigative arm of the U.S. Department of Justice. The FBI investigates violations of the laws of the United States. The agency has jurisdiction over cases that involve illegal drug dealing, terrorism, white collar crimes, and organized crime. In addition, the FBI investigates some kinds of kidnapping, theft from the government, espionage (spying), and hijacking.

The FBI is a fact-finding agency. Special agents uncover information about violations of federal laws. They collect evidence in cases where the U.S. government is or may be an interested party. The FBI then reports its findings to the Justice Department.

The Central Intelligence Agency also is a fact-finding agency. Its members coordinate the nation's intelligence activities. The CIA collects, evaluates, and disseminates foreign intelligence that directly affects national security. It analyzes data from all over the world that might affect the interests of the United States. The CIA provides the President and other policymakers with information they need to establish foreign policy.

Both agencies hire men and women with college degrees in a variety of subject areas.

CAREERS WITH THE FEDERAL BUREAU OF INVESTIGATION

The FBI was established in 1908 as the Bureau of Investigation. In addition to investigating crimes, the bureau acts as a resource and clearinghouse for local and state law-enforcement agencies throughout the United States. The FBI maintains forensic laboratories, fingerprint files, and a National Crime Information Center. Each of these divisions provides law-enforcement officials with information they need to solve crimes.

FBI headquarters is in Washington, D.C., and the bureau has 59 field offices throughout the United States.

Fingerprinting

The FBI currently has on file more than 178 million sets of fingerprints, the largest collection in the world. As a result the agency has been able to house criminal investigation data and identification data on missing persons. Through a service called the International Exchange of Fingerprints, the FBI can exchange identification data with the law-enforcement agencies of more than eighty foreign countries.

The prints of arrested persons, aliens, government job applicants, and military personnel form the large part of the FBI fingerprint records. In addition, many citizens voluntarily submit their fingerprints for personal identification reasons.

The responsibility for submitting complete and up-to-date information concerning the disposition of an arrest lies with the agency submitting the fingerprint card. The FBI strongly urges all police agencies submitting arrest cards to submit a fixed disposition of the case for the completion of the FBI records.

If an individual is being sought by local police for committing a crime, a stop is placed against the fugitive's fingerprints in the FBI Identification Division. The local police are immediately notified of the receipt of any additional fingerprints. The fugitive's name and identification data are also entered in the National Crime Information Center.

Apprehension of Criminals
The FBI laboratory employs specialists trained in many branches of scientific crime detection. They examine and analyze specimens of evidence submitted by agents and by local law-enforcement agencies. Precision instruments and chemical and other processes are utilized in the examination and analysis of bullets, fibers, bloodstains, and other substances.

On the basis of evidence supplied by the FBI, the U.S. government has secured about 14,000 convictions of offenders during recent years, and the identification facilities of the FBI were used to locate more than 33,000 fugitives from justice. The FBI uses many different means to capture criminals.

During the past years, television has been broadcasting shows dealing with law enforcement. Recently there have been such shows as "Rescue 911," "COPS," and "America's Most Wanted." On the latter, the police and FBI agents ask the public's help in finding criminals who are on the run. A reenactment of the crime is shown, along with a photograph and description of the criminal. As a result many men and women who have been running from the law have been turned in by viewers, who are often friends and neighbors of the fugitives.

National Crime Information Center
The National Crime Information Center (NCIC) is a computerized information system established by the FBI as a service to all criminal justice agencies, local, state, and federal. The NCIC stores documented information on missing persons, stolen property, wanted

persons, and criminal histories of persons arrested and fingerprinted for serious offenses. This information can be instantly retrieved over a vast communications network through the use of telecommunication equipment located in criminal justice agencies in the United States, Canada, and Puerto Rico.

JOBS WITH THE FBI

The FBI offers jobs in a variety of areas, including both Special Agent Careers and Non-agent Technical Careers. All FBI employees must be prepared to work overtime, at night, or on weekends. In addition, all employees are required to take drug tests prior to employment.

Special Agent Careers

Special Agents with the FBI must be between the ages of 23 and 35. They must be citizens of the United States or its territories. They must possess keen analytical skills and the ability to make sound, independent decisions.

Agents must be willing to work anywhere within the United States or its territories. They must be in excellent physical condition and may not possess a disability that might limit their using firearms or taking part in raids or risky assignments.

Applicants are required to pass a physical examination. They must pass a vision test and a hearing test. Applicants may be disqualified from consideration if they have a felony or a major misdemeanor on their record.

There are five Special Agent entry programs for which applicants must meet specific requirements:

- Law
- Accounting
- Language

- Engineering/Science
- Diversified

To enter the Law program, a candidate must have a degree from an accredited law school and two years of undergraduate training at a resident college or university. The Accounting program requires a bachelor's degree with a major in accounting from an accredited college or university. In addition, the applicant must be eligible to take the Certified Public Accountant examination.

Those interested in entering the Language program may have a bachelor's degree in any subject area, but they must be fluent in one or more foreign languages. Applicants for the Engineering/Science program must have at least a bachelor's degree in electrical, mechanical, or computer science engineering or one of a variety of physical science–related subjects.

For the Diversified program, an applicant must have either a bachelor's degree and a minimum of three years' full-time work experience, or a graduate degree and two years' full-time work experience.

Non-Agent Technical Career Paths

A number of positions are available with the FBI that support the activities of the Special Agents: clerks, typists, stenographers, and receptionists. Most of these support jobs are at FBI Headquarters in Washington, D.C. They require U.S. citizenship and good health.

TRAINING FOR A SPECIAL AGENT CAREER

Each newly appointed Special Agent receives about sixteen weeks of training at the FBI Academy at the U.S. Marine Corps base in Quantico, Virginia, before being assigned to a field office. During this period, agents receive intensive training in defense tactics, use of firearms, and physical fitness. Agents are thoroughly schooled in federal criminal law and procedures, FBI rules and regulations, fingerprinting, and investigatory work. Agents receive regular salaries while in training.

After being assigned to a field office, the new agent usually works closely with an experienced agent for about two weeks before handling any assignments independently. The following chart is used by the Bureau for physical fitness testing.

NEW AGENTS' PHYSICAL FITNESS TESTS AND RATING SCALE

MEN		WOMEN	
Pull-Ups		**Modified Pull-Ups**	
Number		Number	
Completed	Points	Completed	Points
2–3	1	10–11	1
4–5	2	12–13	2
6–7	3	14–15	3
Pull-Ups		**Modified Pull-Ups**	
Number		Number	
Completed	Points	Completed	Points
8–9	4	16–17	4
10–11	5	18–19	5
12–13	6	20–21	6
14–15	7	22–23	7
16–17	8	24–25	8
18–19	9	26–27	9
20 or more	10	28 or more	10
Push-Ups		**Push-Ups**	
Number		Number	
Completed	Points	Completed	Points
25–30	1	14–17	1
31–35	2	18–21	2

36–40	3	22–25	3
41–45	4	26–29	4
46–50	5	30–33	5
51–55	6	34–37	6
56–60	7	38–41	7
61–65	8	42–45	8
66–70	9	46–49	9
71 or more	10	50 or more	10

Sit-Ups

Number Completed	Points	Number Completed	Points
46–51	1	46–51	1
52–57	2	52–57	2
58–63	3	58–63	3
64–69	4	64–69	4
70–75	5	70–75	5
76–81	6	76–81	6
82–87	7	82–87	7
88–93	8	88–93	8
94–99	9	94–99	9
100 or more	10	100 or more	10

120-Yard Shuttle Run

Time	Points	Time	Points
25.1–26.0	1	28.1–29.0	1
24.6–25.0	2	27.6–28.0	2
24.1–24.5	3	27.1–27.5	3
23.6–24.0	4	26.6–27.0	4
23.2–23.5	5	26.1–26.5	5
22.8–23.1	6	25.6–26.0	6
22.4–22.7	7	25.1–25.5	7
22.0–22.3	8	24.6–25.0	8
21.6–21.9	9	24.1–24.5	9
21.5 or less	10	24.0 or less	10

Two-Mile Run

Time	Points	Time	Points
15:49–16:30	1	17:56–18:45	1

15:24–16:48	2	17:21–17:55	2
14:55–15:23	3	17:01–17:20	3
14:26–14:54	4	16:31–17:00	4
13:57–14:25	5	15:51–16:30	5
13:28–13:56	6	15:31–15:50	6
12:59–13:27	7	15:01–15:30	7
12:30–12:58	8	14:31–15:00	8
12:01–12:29	9	13:46–14:30	9
12:00 or less	10	13:45 or less	10

INCOME AND ADVANCEMENTS

The pay scale for jobs with the federal government is a graded scale, from 1 (lowest) to 18 (highest). The entry-level salary for a Special Agent is $28,322; this is a grade 10 job. Under specific conditions, agents may receive overtime pay of up to about $5,000 a year. Agents can receive pay increases within their grade if their work performance is satisfactory. They advance in grade as they gain experience.

The following is a limited example of the government pay scale:

FEDERAL GOVERNMENT PAY SCALE

Grade Step	1	2	3
GS–1	11,015	11,383	11,749
GS–2	12,385	12,679	13,090
GS–3	13,515	13,966	14,417
GS–4	15,171	15,677	16,183
GS–5	16,973	17,539	18,105

You can move across the scale. This would be a pay increase within grade. Or you can move up the scale to the next grade. As you can see from the chart, you increase your salary more quickly by moving up the scale instead of across.

Non-agent Technical Career paths have a variety of pay levels. Entry-level salaries depend on education and experience.

CAREERS WITH THE CENTRAL INTELLIGENCE AGENCY

The CIA was created in 1947. Its members provide information about trends and current events in other countries. CIA agents gather information about military, political, and economic conditions. National security often depends on information that U.S. intelligence officers supply.

Jobs with the CIA

The Central Intelligence Agency is divided into four major components called Directorates. The Directorate of Operations collects foreign intelligence. The Directorate of Science and Technology designs and operates advanced technical collection systems. The Directorate of Intelligence analyzes information and reports findings, and the Directorate of Administration provides support services for the other three Directorates.

The CIA offers careers in the following occupational categories:

Career Trainee	Personnel (General)
Political Science	General Administration
Economics	Accounting (Budget)
Intelligence Production	Engineering
Military Intelligence	Legal
Geography	Medical
History	Physical Science
Psychology	Library Science
Cartography	Mathematics

Sociology   Logistics
Linguistics   Printing

Qualifications, Education, and Training

General qualifications for working for the CIA include good character, intelligence, and resourcefulness. The agency also looks for people with a willingness to accept responsibility and a strong motivation for public service. Applicants should be willing to work overseas if necessary and must be aware that their work must often remain anonymous. Some CIA undercover agents live under assumed names and changed identities.

Although many people apply for CIA jobs, about 80 percent of applicants never get as far as an interview. The few who make it past the interview must take a lie detector test. If they pass that, they are required to take a physical exam.

United States citizenship is required. An undergraduate or graduate degree in an appropriate field is necessary, and related work experience is a plus.

Some colleges and universities take part in a cooperative education program with the CIA. Interested undergraduates who are majoring in such fields as engineering, physics, computer science, mathematics, business administration, or accounting may spend part of their time in a cooperative work/study program. The CIA also has a summer intern program available to a limited number of graduate students. Foreign language ability is useful but not essential for this program.

Applicants for clerical positions must meet the basic requirements for specific jobs and must take an aptitude test. A background security investigation is made on all accepted applicants before they are assigned to duty. Because this investigation takes time, applicants should apply well in advance of the time they wish to start working.

Potential and Advancement

Although the CIA employs a wide variety of people in many fields, active recruitment for specific jobs varies from year to year.

The CIA offers advancement opportunities to all employees. Formal on-the-job training is available during early and mid-career stages, and professional-level training is given within the CIA and also at other government training establishments, colleges, and universities.

For clerical employees, the CIA's Office of Training offers courses in administrative procedures, writing, employee development, and supervision and management. Off-campus courses are offered by some universities and by specialized schools at CIA headquarters. Tuition costs for approved job-related courses are paid by the CIA. Foreign language study is provided for those who are to serve overseas.

Salaries

Employees of the CIA are paid according to the federal government scale. Starting salaries for employees with bachelor's degrees are around $21,000 to $23,000. For beginning employees with master's degrees, the pay ranges from $23,284 to $28,322. Starting salaries for doctors (both PhDs and MDs) and lawyers fall between $28,322 and $52,406.

Additional Sources of Information

For further information about employment with either the Federal Bureau of Investigation or the Central Intelligence Agency, write the agencies directly:

Central Intelligence Agency
Personnel Representative
PO Box 1925
Department S, Room 4N20
Washington, DC 20013

Federal Bureau of Investigation
Applicant Coordinator
10th and Pennsylvania Avenue, NW
Washington, DC 20520

6

Secret Service Agents

Secret Service agents are a dedicated, highly trained group of men and women who are best known for protecting our government leaders from acts of terrorism or attempts at assassination. In addition to this role, Secret Service agents also are responsible for investigating cases of counterfeiting and forgery.

The Secret Service field is unique and interesting, but jobs in this area are very difficult to get. Applicants must go through months, even years, of interviews, examinations, and background checks. Even when all this probing is complete, the applicant is not guaranteed a job immediately. He or she must then wait for a job opening.

The service includes more than 1,900 special agents, who rotate throughout their careers between investigative and protective assignments. Agents are authorized to protect the following:

- The President of the United States and immediate family.
- The Vice President and immediate family or other officer in order of succession to the Presidency.
- The President-elect, Vice President-elect, and immediate families.
- Former Presidents and their spouses for life,

except that protection of spouse terminates in the event of remarriage.
- Children of former Presidents until the age of sixteen.
- Major Presidential and Vice Presidential candidates and, within 120 days of the Presidential election, the spouses of such candidates.
- Visiting heads of foreign states and their spouses traveling with them.
- Distinguished foreign visitors to the U.S. and official representatives of the U.S. performing special missions abroad.

How Protection Works

When a person needing protection plans to visit a city or town, a lead advance agent is assigned to draw up a security plan. Let's say that Princess Caroline of Monaco is planning to make a stop in Los Angeles to attend a charity ball. Plans for her arrival would begin months earlier.

The Secret Service would want to know every detail, such as what route she would be traveling, where she would be staying, and even where her table would be located at the dinner and dance. The lead agent would begin by forming a special team that would work closely together throughout the planning stages and with other personnel of the nearest district office.

Each site that the Princess was scheduled to visit would be visited ahead of time by this special team. They would determine how many agents would be needed at any given spot, what (if any) equipment would be needed, and other requirements to assure the Princess' safety. Hospitals and evacuation routes would be gone over. Fire, ambulance, and other public service personnel would be alerted to the time of the Princess' arrival.

Agents spend many hours with famous and high-profile people. They are responsible for deterring potential attackers who may lurk in a crowd. Agents are equipped with uniforms and communication systems, such as walkie-talkies, and they do carry firearms. The agents are highly visible. If many security agents are in sight, it is less likely that someone will try to harm the visitor.

Uniformed Division
The men and women of the Secret Service Uniformed Division are an important part of the service's protective program. First established in 1922 as the White House Police, they were renamed in 1977.

Uniformed Division officers in the White House branch are responsible for security at the Executive Mansion and grounds and the Treasury Building and Annex. They screen visitors and patrol the White House grounds.

Their most important job is to see that the President is exposed to as little danger as possible. That involves keeping him away from angry protesters and unruly crowds. It is the agents' responsibility to screen those who will be close to the President. The job requires excellent vision and quick reflexes; so much can happen in just a few seconds that the agent must be alert at all times.

Uniformed security agents also are assigned to protect members of the President's immediate family and the White House. Many agents prefer this duty because less pressure is involved. In protecting the family members, the Secret Service is concerned about the possibility of kidnapping. If there are schoolchildren in the First Family, agents are assigned to accompany them to classes.

Uniformed officers carry out their White House patrol

duties through foot and vehicular patrols, fixed posts, and sometimes canine teams that respond to bomb threats, suspicious packages, and other situations where explosives detection is necessary.

Overseas Presidential or Vice Presidential trips often keep Secret Service agents away from home for four to six weeks at a time. Former agent Marty Venker wrote a book about his experiences protecting the President. Venker wrote, "The hardest part is skipping across time zones. Say you're on a midnight shift to L.A., standing outside the President's door when he's sleeping. As soon as you're off, you board a plane to Boston. You try to get some sleep on the plane, but somebody's always laughing and waking you up. Three time zones later, you land in Boston near 7:00 p.m. You've got only a couple of hours before you're on duty again at midnight. After a while clocks just become decorative objects."*

The Foreign Missions branch of the Uniformed Division safeguards foreign diplomatic missions in the Washington area. Officers maintain foot and cruiser patrol in areas where embassies are located. They are assigned to fixed posts at locations where a threat has been received or at installations of countries involved in tense international situations. This branch also provides security at Blair House when foreign dignitaries are in residence.

Treasury Police Force
The majority of the almost 2,000 agents employed in the Secret Service spend most of their time protecting U.S. currency against counterfeiting. Technological advances in the printing industry have made that job more important than ever. With the printing equipment avail-

---

* *Confessions of an Ex-Secret Service Agent,* by Marty Venker. Donald Fine, New York, 1988.

able today, an experienced printer can turn out money that would fool anyone but an expert.

Treasury security officers are also responsible for security at the main Treasury Building and the Treasury Annex and at the office of the Secretary of the Treasury. They have investigative and special arrest powers in connection with law violations in the Treasury Department, including forgery and fraudulent negotiation of government checks, bonds, and securities. Women are employed in all these categories.

These special agents must deal with everything from counterfeiting run by small-town hoodlums to big-time organized crime. They are closely involved in almost every phase of the Service's protective mission.

In earlier years officers accompanied money shipments from the Bureau of Engraving and Printing, guarded currency in the Treasury Vault, and ensured the security of those doing business in the Treasury Building's cash room. These activities have changed substantially over the years. Today officers of the Treasury Police Force monitor security twenty-four hours a day at the Treasury Building. They also guard the offices of the Secretary of the Treasury and assist in the investigation of crimes.

QUALIFICATIONS EDUCATION, AND TRAINING
OF SPECIAL AGENTS

Special agents may be employed at Secret Service headquarters in Washington, DC, or at one of over 100 field offices throughout the United States.

If you think that you might be interested in this job opportunity, realize the following:

- Special agents must be willing to work wherever they are assigned and are subject to frequent reassignment. Because the protective responsibilities of the Secret Service go around the clock, all agents and officers perform some shift work.

- Competition is tough. Only a limited number of the best-qualified applicants reach the interview stage. Applicants are rated on personal appearance, manner, ability to speak logically and effectively, and ability to adapt.
- Applicants who are selected must be prepared to wait for a vacancy to occur. During this time the applicant's background check is being completed.
- A limited number of the best-qualified applicants receive a series of in-depth interviews and must take a polygraph examination.

Appointees must be less than thirty-five years of age at the time of entrance on duty.

Applicants must have a bachelor's degree or a minimum of three years of experience, of which at least two are in criminal investigation, or a comparable combination of experience and education. College-level study in any major field is acceptable.

Applicants must pass a comprehensive medical examination prior to appointment. Weight must be in proportion to height. Vision requirements are 20/40 in each eye, correctable to 20/20.

Salaries and Advancement

Special agents are appointed on the government pay scale at a GS-5 or a GS-7, depending on experience and education. This means they receive on average $20,000 a year. Eligibility for promotion is based upon on-the-job performance. The full performance level for a special agent is GS-12, between $37,294 and $48,481 a year. Selection for promotion to positions about the GS-12 level is based on merit and on vacancies available.

The Secret Service reports that less than 3 percent of

those who become agents leave before retirement, and most of those drop out of the service within the first year or two. The average agent leaves at the mandatory retirement age, 55. Agents are eligible for retirement at age 50, with 20 years of service.

Benefits
Low-cost health and life insurance may be obtained through federal employee programs. Immediate families may be included in health benefit plans.

Financial protection is provided, without cost, to agents and their families in the event of job-related injury or death.

Annual leave accrues at the rate of 13 to 26 days annually, based on length of employment. Prior federal civilian or military service is creditable.

Sick leave accumulates at the rate of 13 days per year without limit.

Training
Once active duty begins, special agents receive general investigative training at the Federal Law Enforcement Training Center in Brunswick, Georgia, and specialized training at the Secret Service facilities in Washington.

If selected to serve on the force, you will study protective techniques, criminal law, investigative procedures and devices, document and handwriting examinations, first aid, the use of firearms, and various arrest techniques. You will also receive on-the-job training. Advanced in-service training programs continue throughout an agent's career.

Potential for Advancement
From time to time the Service may actively recruit for a specific job category, but for the most part job opportunities are limited. The extremely high public interest

in this work means that only the most highly qualified applicants are considered for appointment. The Secret Service has many more applicants than it has openings, but for those with a strong desire to enter this field, it is worth taking the necessary steps to apply and to be patient in waiting for an opening to occur. You can begin by taking courses in high school such as political science and civics and read additional material that is available regarding jobs in the Secret Service.

The Secret Service promotes women and minorities in all jobs. Many agents were former athletes, and some have law and graduate degrees.

Related specialty occupations include electronics, engineers, communication technicians, computer experts, polygraph examiners, forensic experts, and research psychologists.

Additional Information

Those interested in a career with the Secret Service may obtain more information from the nearest U.S. Office of Personnel Management or from a Secret Service field office. You may also write to:

United States Secret Service
Personnel Division
1800 G Street, NW
Washington, DC 20223

7

Parole and Probation Officers

PAROLE OFFICERS

Parole is a privilege granted to prisoners in recognition of past conduct, both in prison and earlier. You may have heard about a person serving time who was paroled for "good behavior." In essence, it means that the offender was released before his or her prison term had expired. During the parole period, the parolee is required to report from time to time to prison authorities or to a parole officer to whose custody he or she was assigned when released.

Like any social worker, the parole officer is primarily interested in the rehabilitation of the offender. When a parolee engages in illegal activity, it is the parole officer's responsibility to alert the authorities and to protect society.

Violations are based upon the failure of the offender to comply with the conditions of the parole, such as not remaining in a specific place, not reporting to the officer, or committing a new crime or offense. If a violation does occur, the officer may have the parolee arrested and placed in custody pending investigation and a final decision by the parole board.

When the parole officer succeeds in rehabilitating the parolee and removing him or her from a life of crime, he or she is in effect saving society from the further cost of apprehending and detaining the offender again.

Often the parole officer is called upon to play two roles, that of friend and social worker and that of police or detective. It is not an easy job. On one hand the officer tries to help the parolee find a place in society. The officer may be the parolee's only outside contact, and a relationship of friendship and trust can develop between the two. The officer can help the ex-offender find a job or get job training. The officer arranges for welfare or other public assistance for the family if necessary and provides a helping hand in any way possible to aid the parolee. The parole officer's main concern is helping the parolee to go straight instead of returning to a life of crime.

On the other hand, however, the officer also has the duty to watch closely over the parolee and to police his or her activities in the outside world. If the officer suspects that the parolee is violating or planning to violate the conditions of parole, action must be taken. The officer needs to be sure that the parolee is not planning to flee the state or country or engage in any illegal activities.

How Parole Works

To illustrate the parole procedure, the successive steps follow.

- On arrival at jail the inmate is informed of the meaning of parole, how it is earned, and how he or she must behave while on parole. The inmate learns that earning parole requires good behavior and positive effort.
- Institution personnel prepare the inmate's case for the parole hearing. This involves compiling

progress reports, psychological findings, medical reports, and personality evaluations.

- At the parole hearing all the information regarding the prisoner's case is studied. Parole may be approved, denied, or deferred, or no action may be taken.
- If parole is approved, plans are initiated by the board. This involves planning for a home and a job for the offender and the assigning of a parole officer.
- The prisoner is released under the supervision of the parole staff. Conditions are attached, usually that the parolee must report to the parole officer at certain times and that he/she may not leave the state, move to another residence, take another job, or get married or divorced without permission from the parole office or parole board. The parolee is required to lead a law-abiding life and to avoid places and people of questionable character.
- The parole officer make periodic visits to the parolee and checks with other family members, friends, and employer regarding the parolee's behavior and activities. The officer writes a report of the parolee's activities.
- Supervision by the parole officer is gradually eased. There are less frequent visits and reports and fewer restrictions.
- The parolee is discharged from parole either at the expiration of the prison sentence or by action of the parole board prior to the expiration date.
- Certification of rehabilitation is issued by the parole board when the parolee has maintained a satisfactory record for a required term of years after release from confinement.

PROBATION OFFICER

The probation officer supervises the offender for the probation period, which is fixed by the court and by law. During this period, the offender must not commit a criminal offense and must report to the probation office at regular intervals. In the course of his or her work, the probation officer deals with teachers, chaplains, rabbis, social workers, counselors, employers, and community organizations.

This job requires initiative and an understanding of human relationships. It is the officer's job to treat and help the offender, not to judge him or her. Because it is possible that the offender may repeat his or her acts, the probation officer must be on guard. Restrictions are therefore placed upon the offender's activities during the probation period.

Working with Juveniles

Perhaps one of the most important areas of work of the probation officer is with juveniles. Officers deal with juvenile delinquents and first offenders, who are often released by the court subject to supervision, instead of being sentenced to jail or prison.

The officer tries to establish a rapport with the children and teenagers who have been in trouble with the law. He or she discusses the juveniles' problems and tries to get them back on the right track.

Probation officers do this through a process of reeducation and redirection. Besides monitoring the juvenile's activities, the officer writes a report for the court on his/her progress. The following are areas that the officer delves into when writing the report:

- *A description of circumstances*, such as what the juvenile did that got him in trouble with the law.

Was the child placed in detention? What is the child's attitude toward his/her situation?

- *A record of information* about the child's parents and immediate family. What is the father like? What is the mother like? How do the siblings in the home get along?
- *Child's social and development history.* Does the child have any physical or mental handicaps? Are there any unusual circumstances in the child's development rate? How does he or she relate to friends? What type of discipline is used in the home? Is there a clash of methods used?
- *Education progress and maturity.* How is the child doing in school? Does he get along with his teachers and those in authority? Is he or she involved in sports? What type of friends does the child have?
- *Work history.* What kinds of jobs has the child worked at? Did he or she get along with the employer and the other employees? Was he or she on time and responsible in the job?

The probation officer takes everything into consideration when writing a report. If the home conditions are less than adequate and there are financial problems, it will affect the child if placed back in the home while on probation. The probation officer also makes recommendations as to what steps may be taken to help the child in the future.

The reports are objective and are intended to aid the court in making an intelligent disposition of a case. The officer is not required to secure evidence as to the guilt or innocence of a person. However, if negative evidence is brought to the officer's attention, it should be reported to the authorities.

A probation officer's caseload can sometimes be a

hindrance to the effectiveness of his or her work. Many parole and probation officers must keep track of up to 100 assigned cases, which makes it difficult to give each person the attention and help that are necessary.

The rewards are great, however, when a parole or probation officer is able to help someone get back on the right track. By lending an understanding ear and offering assistance, the officer can be the means of changing a person's life for the better.

Qualifications, Education, and Training

A number of parole and probation officers come from the ranks of police officers. People who work in this field need training and experience in sociology, psychology, and criminology. Those who start out as police officers usually acquire additional training in these fields through college courses.

Requirements vary. Some states require a degree, sometimes in a specific field. Personal characteristics of understanding, objectivity, good judgment, and patience are necessary. Good communication skills and the ability to motivate people are very important. High school courses should include the social sciences, English, and history. A bachelor's degree in criminal justice, the social sciences, or a related field is required in nearly all systems.

Potential for Advancement

The demand for qualified parole and probation officers is especially great in large metropolitan areas. The field is open to women and all minorities. Some officers advance by acquiring additional education that qualifies them for positions in other areas of law enforcement.

Requirements

When a position is open, a job announcement is prepared. The announcement contains everything an applicant needs to know about the job, including title, duties, and salary. It describes the work, the location, the education and experience requirements, the kind of exam to be given, and the system of rating. It states which application form is to be filled out and where and when to file it.

The following are places where information about careers in probation and parole can be obtained.

- The offices of the State Employment Service. (You can find the address of the one nearest you in the telephone directory.)
- The state Civil Service Commission. (Address your inquiry to the capital city of your state.)
- The city Civil Service Commission, Department of Personnel.
- The municipal building and the library.
- The newspaper. (Many newspapers run a section on regional Civil Service news.)

Income

The salaries for both probation and parole officers fall within a wide range, from about $17,000 to around $53,000. Much depends on the area of the country in which you are working and on the amount of education you have received.

Federal probation and parole officers normally start on the government pay scale at a GS-9 rating, which is between $25,717 and $33,430 a year. After one year, probation and parole officers may advance to a GS-11 rating, which pays between $31,116 and $40,449 annually.

Additional Sources of Information

Those interested in obtaining additional information about careers as probation or parole officers may write to the following organizations:

American Correctional Association
8025 Laurel Lakes Court
Laurel, MD 20707-5075

Association of Paroling Authorities International
c/o The Council of State Governments
District of Columbia Board of Parole
PO Box 11910
Lexington, KY 40578

8

Security Guards

Careers in security involve the protection of public and private property. Security guards protect property such as office buildings, airports, banks, and educational institutions against theft, fire, vandalism, and illegal entry.

Depending on where they work, security guards may have a variety of titles. Those who work at bars or dance clubs often are called "bouncers." Guards who patrol airports might be called "airline security representatives," and those who work at shopping malls would be called "merchant patrollers."

Security guards may be employed at any time during the day or night. Many guards work during normal business hours in areas where there is a good deal of public contact. A large number of guards patrol buildings and grounds at night or on weekends when they see few, if any, members of the public.

Day guards usually are employed by such places as libraries, museums, art galleries, and other public buildings. Night guards generally work at industrial plants, construction sites, or defense operations.

All security jobs require the same basic skills, but the different environments in which the guards work add variety to the field. Security guards may find themselves in very different situations at different times, and they need to be prepared to deal with those situations:

I saved a life, and it's something I will never forget. I was working as a guard in a Chicago high-rise back in 1984. A fire broke out on the 18th floor. I saw the smoke on one of my desk monitors; then I heard the alarms go off. It looked like the smoke was coming from a back storage room and moving into the work area, but the alarms malfunctioned and did not go off. When I looked at my number three monitor for that floor, employees were still working at their desks.

I immediately called up and told them to get off the floor, and I saw on the monitor that they were running out to the stairwells. One woman was left behind; she was in the restroom, I guess, when everyone else was alerted about the fire. When she came out into the office area and saw smoke coming down the hallway, she panicked and ran into her boss's office, shutting the door behind her.

The fire department had not yet arrived, so I left my station and went up the 18th floor. I was pounding on the door. The woman had locked it and would not let me in. I was worried we would both be overcome by the smoke if I didn't act quickly. So I kicked in the door and pulled the woman down 17 flights of stairs.

When I got back to my station, a group of my fellow security guards started clapping and whistling. They had seen everything on the monitor at my desk. I was the hero of the day.

—Micky, 42

I work as a guard at the front gate of a stereo manufacturing plant. All parts from shipping and receiving have to be cleared by me. Besides having the responsibility for factory parts, I also am on the lookout for employee theft, which happens more often than you would think.

In the past three years that I have been working here, I have had my life threatened, been set up by another employee, and been held up at gunpoint. I once broke up an inside job that had speaker parts going out the door in empty trash barrels. I made enemies of the guys that tried to pull it off, but those kind of people I don't count as friends anyway.

The company management was overjoyed. I saved them a bundle of money and got a bonus from the president of the company and from my boss at the security company, too. I like working in security. It has its moments.

—Patrick, 29

I work as a guard at a museum. People always ask me if they can change jobs with me. They kid around because my job seems so easy. My job is not extremely difficult; a few problems have happened on the job, but they were not that serious. Our museum has an elaborate electronic security system. So if anything suspicious happens, the police are alerted immediately.

My job is mainly to direct people, answer questions as best I can, and make sure everyone is out and that things are put away for closing time. I like this job because I get to meet people from all over the country. I find that people in general are pretty good-natured—especially children. I like children, and our museum has a separate section for young people. They are always asking me where something is located or how something works.

I'm working here part time and attending classes at the university in preparation for a career in law enforcement. This job is great experience for whatever area of law enforcement I choose to go into in the future.

—Karen, 22

People often think security officers just sit behind a desk and watch a monitor, or check incoming and outgoing supplies of a company. But the job requires more than that. Guards must think on their feet. They must always be alert and on the lookout for suspicious characters or circumstances.

A guard stationed at a bank should not simply ignore a suspicious person who is hanging out in the lobby. The guard should take note of the person's appearance and be ready to detain the person if the situation calls for that kind of action. Certain questions should immediately be asked by a guard when he or she notices something out of the ordinary.

- Why does the person appear nervous when entering a place of business and asking to see a particular employee?
- Why is the person here after hours without an appointment, asking to see the head of a certain department?
- Why is a bank customer asking questions about where the money is kept or about inside banking procedures?
- Why is a person demanding entry into a secured

area when he or she is not on the list of people to be admitted?

Some security jobs may require more observation than others. In addition to observation, guards may perform any number of tasks, depending on where they are employed. Some guards enforce the rules, give directions, inspect packages, or sign people in and out. Others work with undercover detectives to watch for theft by customers or store employees. Guards keep traffic moving, direct people to their seats, and eject unruly spectators. In larger organizations a single security guard may be placed in charge of the guard force.

Bank Guard

Guarding banks is a high-profile and somewhat high-pressure job. You must always be alert until the moment you are relieved by another guard. Anything can happen in a split second, and the guard's eyes and ears must always be attuned to the goings-on inside the bank. If you choose this career, be prepared to be asked questions, such as the location of the loan department or the place for credit card applications. You will also have to deal with customers' complaints, from the time it took them to move through the line, to the paintings that hang on the walls. A bank security guard must be courteous and listen patiently to everything.

Campus Security Officer

The police department does not have the manpower to supervise many areas of campus property. Guards are hired to patrol traffic on the grounds as well as handle any disturbances thay may occur. Because of the large numbers of students massed in one area, it isn't unusual for fights to break out or rowdiness to occur. Campus guards must have patience, tact, and courtesy but not be afraid to use force if necessary to insure the safety of the students and the administration.

Corporate Security Officer

One of the best places to obtain good training is the guard force of a corporate or industrial organization. Guards in this field are responsible for overall policing and procedures. They cover such matters as inspection, disaster and emergency preparedness, and employee investigation and clearance.

Corporate security guards are responsible for the control of entrances and exits to the building. The authority to arrest or to search and seize is subject to local police control. Each state, city, and community varies in regulations regarding security. Corporate security guards usually are supplied with uniforms, badges, and equipment.

This job requires the ability to think and act quickly and to make judgment decisions on the spot. Guards must maintain order and enforce company regulations. They are also expected to watch for fires and suspicious persons and to guard the company against material loss.

Hospital Security Officer

Hospital guards protect property, prevent crime, watch for fires, and patrol floors. Following are some of the duties of hospital guards:

- Insure safety of personnel leaving or arriving at odd hours.
- Guard against kidnapping of babies on the maternity floor.
- Direct visitors.
- Discourage outside solicitors.
- Handle deliveries of medical supplies and equipment.
- Maintain daily log of activities.

Hospital guards are protective agency employees. They are uniformed and armed.

Armored Car Guards

Armored car guards protect money and valuables in transit. They are often the target of robberies and therefore are trained in the use of firearms.

Armored car guards must know who remains inside the car and exactly how many paces he or she stands from the person next to him or her. Every move is thought out, planned, and rehearsed. There is even a sequence for reentering the vehicle.

To guarantee a superior security force, strict screening methods are required. Private security companies use careful means to insure that guards are of the highest quality. Their backgrounds are checked, and drug tests are often required.

Government Guards

Government guards patrol all types of federal properties throughout the U.S., protecting them, their contents, and their occupants. Guards prevent unauthorized entry to restricted areas and unauthorized removal of property from all areas. They maintain their posts, control traffic, and take immediate action against hazards that may cause damage or injury. Guards also make arrests for cause and write required reports.

The job requires moderate to great physical exertion and sometimes courteous contact with the public. All people are considered for this employment without regard to race, religion, sex, national origin, political affiliation, or any other non-merit factor. Being a veteran is an asset. You must also be mentally and emotionally stable, a citizen of the United States, and eighteen years of age. You must pass a physical exam and a background check.

To apply for this position, obtain a copy of the pamphlet that is published by the U.S. Civil Service Commission.

Movie Studio Security Guard

Mario is a 55-year-old security guard who works at a major movie studio in Los Angeles. He agreed to answer some questions regarding his job:

Q: Can you describe your duties?

A: They vary. I oversee and supervise the guards at their respective gates, I do on-site investigations of accidents that occur on the set, and I oversee safety and security procedures at the studio.

Q: Do you feel that this is a rewarding or challenging job at this point in your career?

A: Yes, it is.

Q: In what way?

A: It goes beyond the simple situation of the guard sitting at the gate and checking who goes in and who goes out. I am now involved in the administrative aspect of the job, which determines policies and procedures to avoid any hazardous situations on the lot.

Q: While you have been working at the studio, have you ever had occasion to draw your gun, or have you found yourself in a dangerous situation?

A: We in the security staff on the set do not carry guns.

Q: Can you remember a time when you felt that you had to rise to the occasion, so to speak?

A: There are times, usually when there is a union problem that results in pickets about the studio lot. Usually some people try to keep others from entering the lot, and that does get difficult to handle, because tempers flare and I have conflicting interests. One is trying to control the ongoing operations of the lot, and the other is trying to keep the strike situation under control. Sometimes very heated arguments transpire.

Q: Before you came to work at the studio, what were your earlier jobs as a guard?

A: After leaving high school, I was offered a job as a bouncer at a nightclub in Anaheim. It consisted of checking out IDs, making sure that the staff was adequately protected, and making sure that no problems occurred inside or outside the establishment. After that I began to get interested in security, in the procedures and such. After a short time I was elevated to chief doorman and stayed in that position for two and a half years. I obtained my guard's license and the appropriate baton and mace licenses. From there I got a job at a studio from contacts that I made in the entertainment industry. I provided security at the lounge. Not long after, I heard of an opening at a studio near my home, and I jumped at the chance. I worked hard and was able to advance to different positions within the studio to the point where I am now, advisor on all policy and procedures. I have a staff of twelve beneath me.

Q: Is there any advice you can give young adults who are interested in entering the field of security?

A: Anyone intending to enter the security field should remember first and most important to have a *clean record*. That includes staying clear of drugs and any other unlawful activity. This will be thoroughly checked by any employer looking for security personnel. Second, you must have the proper training. A number of schools are available. Attend a reputable school, obtain your baton license, your mace license, and if you are interested in a job within a particular company, find out their requirements and satisfy those requirements before you apply. That way, you are almost assured of landing a job over someone who has to start fullfilling the requirements you have already completed.

Q: What is your opinion on future opportunities for security jobs?

A: There will always be opportunities for security guards. They have a tendency to be somewhat transitory and therefore there is a higher than average replacement factor. Normally, applicants start working as guards, then become supervisors, then advance to directors of security at different companies. When they reach that point they find that it is a very comfortable job; it is a fun job because there are always new and different situations facing you.

Q: On a final note, as a top man in the security field, what would you look for in hiring a person for a job?

A: I would look for a clean appearance and a clean record, along with a desire to succeed in the job.

Job Requirements

Although there are no educational requirements for security guards, many are college-educated and highly professional. Often they are trained in CPR, basic fighting techniques, and loss-prevention measures.

Most employers prefer high school graduates. They require general good health, emotional stability, and the ability to follow instructions. Applicants with police or military experience improve their chances of employment.

Most employers require that their workers submit to drug testing. Some want applicants to take polygraph tests or written examinations. For some jobs you may need a driver's permit; for others you may have to be bonded (meaning that someone guarantees to make good on any damage or loss caused by an action of yours).

Entering the Field

Usually people interested in security work apply directly to the security companies. Some jobs may be available through state or private employment services.

To prepare for a job in the security field you can take courses that will enable you to better understand federal laws, state statutes, and city ordinances. Communications skills are helpful.

You may want to take a part-time job to get acquainted with security work. Apply for work at sporting events, such as soccer, baseball, or even wrestling matches. Offer your help to security agencies in jobs such as secretarial, bookkeeping, or vehicle repair. These support jobs will acquaint you with the field and allow you to observe it from a bit of a distance.

Training

Although many employers give newly hired guards brief instruction before they start a job, some employers require extensive formal training. Guards at nuclear plants, for example, may receive several months of training.

During training, security guards may be taught public

relations, first aid, drug control, communications skills, and firearms use. Other areas of training could include how to operate alarm systems and electronic security equipment, how to handle emergencies and evacuations, and how to spot and deal with security problems.

Women in Security

Female security guards are employed in all areas. They are used in surveillance operations and as security in public assemblies, sports events, industrial plants, and hospitals. Female security officers are a part of every protection agency's staff.

Minorities

All minorities are encouraged to apply for positions in security, and they do in fact hold a large number of security jobs. The International Organization of Black Security Executives is dedicated to promoting opportunities in security management for minorities. The IOBS is a nonprofit organization that shares expertise and information regarding security jobs throughout the nation. Each year members put on programs at black colleges and universities to inform students about private security careers.

Salaries

A security guard's pay depends on his or her level of training and experience, and on the type and location of the employer. Newly hired guards in the federal government, for example, earn between $13,500 and $15,200 a year; the average is about $19,200.

Hourly wages range from about $4.75 to about $12.00. The average hourly pay for a guard is about $6.25. Those employed in manufacturing plants are paid the highest wages, while those employed by security agencies generally start at or slightly above minimum wage.

Guards employed by smaller institutions receive periodic salary increases, but advancement usually is limited. Larger organizations use a military type of ranking that offers advancement in both position and salary.

In-house guards enjoy higher earnings and benefits and greater job security than contract security guards. In-house guards also usually receive more training.

Some persons with guard experience transfer to police jobs that offer higher pay and greater opportunities for advancement. Guards with some college education may advance to jobs that involve administrative duties. A few guards with management skills open their own contract security agencies.

Job Outlook

Currently, about 883,000 people are employed as security guards in the United States. The demand for guards is expected to be strong through the end of the decade.

Many guards are older, retired or semiretired, and turnover in the field is rapid. New personnel are always needed to fill these empty positions.

Additional Information

For additional information about a career in the security field, visit your local library or write to:

International Association of Security Service
PO Box 8202
Northfield, IL 60093

International Union of Security Officers
2404 Merced Street
San Leandro, CA 94577

9

Private Investigator

Private investigators perform a wide variety of duties. They work for insurance companies, law firms, and private individuals. The life of a private investigator can be exciting. Many investigators own their own business and employ a staff such as a secretary and an assistant to help in the search for documents and to deliver court records to attorneys and businesses.

Usually a great deal of travel is involved in this profession. Your may be called upon to locate a witness and bring him in for an upcoming trial, or to perform a sub rosa investigation, that is, to watch a person without that person's knowledge.

TYPES OF PRIVATE INVESTIGATION JOBS

Insurance Company Investigator

Insurance companies often hire private detectives to research possible false claims. Identifying false claims saves money for the company and, in turn, for those the company insures.

Perhaps a person is claiming injury to his back. He slipped and fell at a restaurant and is making a claim for compensation to the restaurant's insurance company. Not only is he looking to be paid for his injury, but also

105

ASSIGNMENT SHEET

DATE REC'D: August 3, 1994   FROM: Samantha R. Robbins

OF: American Casualty

Insurance Co.

CLAIM #	POLICY #	EFFECTIVE DATES	OTHER
750613	RSR658000	5/7/93 to 5/7/94	

INSURED: Marty's Restaurant   INSURED'S ATTY: No attorney

343 North Main St.   involved

Minneapolis,

Minnesota

Tel: 612/555-0907   Tel:

CLAIMANT: Joseph Skinner   CLAIMANT'S ATTY: No attorney

21356 E. 22nd St.   involved

Minneapolis,

Minn. 55406

Tel: Tel:

DATE OF LOSS: 12/22/88   TYPE OF LOSS: Slip and Fall

INCIDENT DESCRIPTION: Joseph Skinner entered Marty's Restaurant at 11:30 a.m. on December 12, 1988. He claims to have slipped on water that was left on the floor in front of the salad bar area. Subject alleges he fell, landing on his back, and sustained injury to his upper and middle back. Paramedics arrived and subject was transported to Northfield Hospital, where he was treated and released.

NEEDS/INSTRUCTIONS: (X) FULL INVESTIGATION

COMMENTS: (If Any) Find out what substance was on the floor area at time of fall; investigate clean-up procedures for restaurant; ask for hospital bills along with any other applicable medical receipts.

1)	Obtain J. Skinner statement	4)	Photos of restaurant floor
2)	Witness statements (if any)	5)	Obtain medical reports
3)	Statement from Manager	6)	Obtain wage loss statement

106

to be reimbursed for the days he had to take off work and for a housekeeper he had to hire to make his meals and take care of him while he was home in bed.

The investigator is called in and asked to check out the facts before any money is paid. The insurance company wants to know how exactly the person fell, what were the contributing factors to the fall, whether the person had a bad back to begin with, and many more details. It wants to determine its liability.

The first thing investigators do when they receive an assignment is to meet with the person who is hiring their services. The detective brings an Assignment Sheet to the meeting and asks questions to clarify the duties required in performing the investigation. The detective wants the names of the parties involved, the names of any witnesses, the date of the incident and, in this case, a statement from the restaurant staff.

After the detective has all the information needed, he or she makes a call to the person making the claim—provided the subject has not hired an attorney. If an attorney has been hired, he or she will deal directly with the insurance company and the investigator. No contact will be permitted with the person filing the claim.

If no attorney has been hired, the investigator and the claimant set a time and place for an interview. The investigator usually brings a camera to photograph a visible injury or the accident area. A tape recorder is used, and a question-and-answer type of interview takes place. The investigator knows that research must be done regarding the incident and that questions must be asked to determine liability. A complete picture must be brought forth, including times, dates, names, and places. In this back-injury case, the investigator might ask:

- What were the weather conditions on the day of the accident?

DATE	ACTIVITY LOG	EXPENSES	TIME
1/7/94	Received file information, called J.		
	Skinner and made appointment for		
	statement and photos of his injury.		.3
1/11/94	Met with J. Skinner, obtained statement		
	regarding fall at restaurant. Obtained		
	medical reports and additional misc.		
	bills.		2.0
1/13/94	Called Marty's Restaurant, spoke with		
	manager, Ron Miller. Made		
	arrangements to inspect area and		
	speak to clean-up personnel.		.2
1/15/94	Drove to Marty's Restaurant, spoke to		
	Ron Miller and cashier who was		
	witness to incident. Obtained		
	statement from Miller and cashier		
	Sarah Downey. Photographed floor		
	area.		2.5
1/19/94	Firest report to insurance company		
	regarding findings to date.		.5
		Total Hours . . .	5.5

- What kind of shoes was the subject wearing when he slipped and fell?
- Was the subject on any type of medication that may have caused him to be off-balance?
- Were there any warning signs about the condition of the floor on the day in question?

Once the facts have been determined, the investigator writes a report to the insurance company. The tape-recorded statement is transcribed by the secretary or an outside typing service. The photographs are developed and mounted on a photo sheet. Diagrams are included, as well as the investigator's comments on the facts surrounding the claim. An activity log is filled in, showing the work the investigator has performed. The complete file is copied, and the original is sent to the insurance company, usually within thirty days.

"Sub Rosa" Investigating

When the opposing sides of a court case (the plaintiff's and the defendant's attorneys) set out to determine who is liable for an accident or injury, they often hire investigators to determine the exact extent of the injury sustained.

The investigator is hired to observe the injured party without his or her being aware of the surveillance. The procedure is allowed by law, as long as the investigator does not interrupt, interfere, or cause any nuisance to the person. A sub rosa investigation allows the investigator to see the person bowling when he or she claims to be bedridden with a sprained back, on watch a person mow his or her lawn when he or she claims to be in a wheelchair with a broken leg.

In a sub rosa investigation, the PI determines where the person resides and where he or she works. The investigator identifies any outside activities in which the

OWNER Bradford Investigations   IDENTIFICATION NUMBER CIC 600

LOCATION   Marty's Restaurant

COMPANY CLAIM NUMBER   750613   POLICY NUMBER   RSR65800

FILM   35MM   POLAROID ☐   NEGATIVE ☐   DATE TAKEN   1/6/94

PICTURE # 1
DESCRIPTION

Subject J. Skinner

bruises to middle

and lower back

PICTURE # 2
DESCRIPTION

Inside floor

area of Marty's

Restaurant

Location of

claimant's fall

person is involved. The PI may take photographs, but he or she is not allowed to climb fences or peer through windows to gain this information. Any discrepancies identified by the private investigator are filed in an official report.

Missing Persons Search

Individuals sometimes hire private investigators to locate missing family members. The fee is agreed upon before any work is initiated. An investigator's fee to locate a person can be as little at $10 to $15 an hour plus expenses, or as much as $200 or more.

A private investigator hired to find a missing person is virtually on call. Phone calls come in at all hours of the day and night. People that the investigator speaks to during the day may remember additional information and want to relate it as soon as possible. A great deal of travel is involved in the locating of missing persons. One investigator explains:

When I am asked to find someone, I use every available source of information that comes my way. This includes clues that family members drop in the course of a conversation, or recollections of a missing person's past activities, something that may lead me to their present whereabouts.

I also use information from the Department of Motor Vehicles, real estate information, and from the subject's past employers or neighbors.

When I do locate a missing person, I ask the person who hired me what he wants to do. I never take it upon myself to apprehend a person. If I am asked to serve a subpoena, I will. At times I will call in a policeman or the marshal to accompany me to the door. This is when I know I will be met with hostility and I feel the situation might be dangerous.

Each of my cases is different. I feel a sense of satisfaction when I have found a loved one, a friend, or a family member. I like to see people reunited in a happy way. I know I have done my job.

—Ed, 45

The following is an interview with Paul Cohen, coauthor and owner of Cohen & Associates.

Sometimes the "missing person" is a court witness and the private investigator's job is to locate the person so he or she can assist with a trial. The process of litigation may take up to four years. People involved in a case tend to move around, and they become lost in the sense that their addresses are no longer known; some have moved to different states, their phone numbers have changed, etc.

Unless the investigator can secure information such as a social security number or the name and address of a family member, it can be very difficult to find a person who has moved. A private investigator's office often gets calls from attorneys who need a witness immediately but cannot locate him or her.

The investigator's first move might be to check with the Department of Motor Vehicles to locate an automobile registration. Then the investigator might check the voters' registration, the public library for old phone books, fictitious business filings, or criminal cases (in the event that the person is now in prison). Next the private investigator might check with family members, with the post office, and with former neighbors.

Services are being established whereby one can search databases of information to locate missing persons. These computer files enable an investigator to search for information in the comfort of his or her office. The services are still limited, however, and can be quite costly.

Work as a Private Investigator

The life of a private investigator is far from typical. It is different from morning to morning, according to Paul Cohen, owner of the investigation firm Cohen & Associates. The day usually begins earlier than everyone else's and ends later than most. "Normally, one has to get to the office and start on the paperwork," Mr. Cohen says. "By that I mean that you have to keep up with the daily reporting to whoever gave you the assignments, your principals, so that they willl be informed as to how the case or claim is progressing. Without that, your usefulness as a private investigator is limited."

Once the paperwork and dictation of reports is completed, the day must be planned. The plan may consist of outlining the items to be done during the day on the cases or it may just be a geographic outline of the areas to which you must travel and the times of your appointments. "You need to coordinate the times and places to maximize the value of the day," Mr. Cohen says.

When the regular day is over, an investigator checks in with his or her answering service or secretary and gets the day's messages. The calls are returned and the needs or requests of the callers handled at this time. The investigator then tries to complete appointments that he or she was unable to take care of during the day. That may include talking to witnesses who can meet only after working hours. The business day of an investigator can start as early as 7 a.m. and end as late as midnight.

Rewards

The top reward for working as a private investigator, according to Mr. Cohen, is the financial reward. An average investigator in the United States can earn in excess of $35 an hour, plus time and expenses. That can add up to about $50 or $55 an hour. Some investigators charge up to $1,000 for only a few minutes of work.

"Besides the financial rewards, the most rewarding aspect of this job is that I am able to find out the truth without concern for any liability determination," Mr. Cohen says. "My job as an investigator is to determine once and for all what the true facts are. It is irrelevant whether the facts are in favor of one person or another. I derive great personal satisfaction in knowing the truth, as opposed to who is at fault or who is responsible."

Many private investigators like being away from the office during the day. They find sitting in an office all day confining and restricting. They do not enjoy sitting behind a desk and working in accounting or inventory control, seeing the same paperwork and the same people throughout the day. Private investigators may never see the same person or the same claim in a pile of 200 that they are asked to investigate. The facts of one case may be similar to those of another, but the personalities vary from day to day. That variety keeps may PIs enthusiastic about their jobs and always looking forward to the next case.

Drawbacks

Private investigation work is very time-consuming and very stressful. There are limits on the number of cases that you can perform competently. Many investigators take on numerous cases but do not give each case the careful attention it deserves. Others take on too few and give them total attention, but find out that the money runs short and they cannot make an adequate living. A good investigator tries to pace the caseload and plan the work accordingly.

A danger of the job is that it sometimes puts you in unusual situations. If you approach a person with the intention of getting facts for a case, the person may be angry about the case and vent his or her anger or frustration on you. For example, you might be hired to investigate an automobile accident. You may be met with anger and hostility because you represent a law firm or an insurance company, and the parties see you as an enemy.

Another area that may involve danger is process serving, the serving of documents from a law office or court requiring a person's presence for trial or for a deposition. Process serving is usually done by people who are just starting out in the field and may need the hours of work to qualify for a license. On the other hand, it may be done by very experienced people who have a knack for finding people and are hired specifically for the purpose. In my opinion, not a great deal of money is to be made by limiting oneself to process serving. Also, people value their privacy, and when a stranger comes to door and tries to serve them with papers—especially if the case involves anger—the process server immediately becomes the enemy.

Working Conditions

Some private investigators work out of offices in their homes. Others rent office space or work in an office building owned by their employer. PIs are not often placed in life-threatening situations. Most of their activities involve interviewing or observing people, or sifting through a variety of legal records about people.

Certain PI jobs may require visits to city or state government offices, where legal records are kept. Other jobs may require travel throughout the country.

Skills and Requirements

Most private investigation work requires three to four years experience in a city police department or similar work experience. Most states require applicants for a license to have a high school diploma or a GED certificate. Many PIs have some college education.

PIs should be familiar with investigative techniques, the local, state, and federal laws and a variety of research methods. Computer skills are becoming useful. Most business now own personal computers to "write up" reports, and a growing amount of government information is available through computer database access.

Future Outlook

The job outlook for private investigators is very good. A growing number of businesses, hotels, and even restaurants are employing investigators to look for losses from theft and fraud. Some businesses hire PIs to do industrial undercover work. Insurance companies hire investigators to look into disability claims.

Applying for the Job

Perhaps after what you have read, you feel that this career sounds interesting. What next? Start by looking in the newspaper for openings as an investigator's assistant. The ad would probably read something like this:

ASSIST PRIVATE INVESTIGATOR

Locate court records, write reports,
assist P.I. in running of business.
Must have car with insurance.
Contact Ann after 3:00 p.m.

Following are some things that many private investigation firms look for when hiring an employee to assist them in their investigation business.

- Does the applicant appear to have the emotional balance necessary for the job? Does he or she appear to be in control, or seem as though he would come apart under stress?
- Does the applicant appear to have a real interest in working as an investigator? (We often come across people who apply just for the fun of it, for something to do to fill their time. They have no real interest in the job, and it shows in their work performance.)
- Does the applicant appear serious-minded and intelligent? Will he or she be able to weigh the merits of a question before deciding, or make a snap judgment?
- Does he or she show confidence and self-reliance?
- Will the applicant be able to grasp ideas quickly?
- Does the applicant have positive references from past employers or from people in the community who can give a character reference?
- Does he or she have good manners and a pleasant personality? (We always keep in mind that our employees are a reflection of ourselves and our office. A neat and courteous staff is a reflection of a professional business office.)

Experience

Many related jobs can qualify as experience in working toward an investigator's license. Work in library research helps with researching court records and documents. The ability to drive the streets of your city and know how to get from place to place is a plus. It is important to be able to speak with other people in a knowledgeable

117

and polite manner, such as court clerks, legal secretaries, store managers, etc.

It is a sure bet that an investigation firm will hire a less experienced but enthusiastic person over one who has many credits but has a lethargic personality. Investigators come from all walks of life. Students, housewives, and grandmothers have earned the necessary hours to become licensed investigators. After you accumulate your hours, you write to the Department of Consumer Affairs in your state asking for a license application. They will send you an information packet and instructions. Most states require that you pass an exam. Following is the form used by the state of Minnesota for a private detective license. Again, each state varies, so it is advisable to contact your state board to determine what exactly you will need to obtain your license.

STATE OF MINNESOTA

Board of Private Detective and
Protective Agent Services
1246 University Avenue
St. Paul, MN 55104

APPLICATION REQUIREMENTS/PROCEDURES

The licensing requirements and procedures for Private Detectives and Protective Agents are defined in Minnesota State Statutes 326.32 to 326.339. This information sheet summarizes the key requirements and procedures involved. For specific language, refer directly to the statutes.

Definitions regarding the application process can be found in the introductory portion of the statute. Specifically, for identification purposes, the following positions will require that distinctions be made:

APPLICANT—Any individual making application for a private detective or protective agent license on an individual license level.

QUALIFIED REPRESENTATIVE—Refers to the individual to be involved in the day-to-day management and supervision of the licensed activity in a partnership or corporation. This subject is required to meet all qualification standards as dictated by statute.

MINNESOTA MANAGER—If a license applicant is a partnership or corporation, based outside Minnesota, it will require the designation of a Minnesota Manager for any business regularly conducted at a Minnesota office location. The candidate for this position is required to meet the same experience qualifications as the Qualified Representative.

As an introduction to the statute, the following are some of the basic requirements of applicants, qualified representatives, Minnesota managers, and those parties signing the application:

1. Each person signing the application must be at least 18 years of age.
2. Each person must have a record free of felony convictions, and no record of convictions of offenses stipulated in statute.
3. Each license applicant must supply a $10,000 Surety Bond (private detective or protective agent) at the time of application.
4. Each license applicant must supply Proof of Financial Responsibility (options for fulfillment are delineated in statute) at the time of application.
5. Complete required application materials and supporting documents.
6. Be of good character, honesty and integrity.

EXPERIENCE—The applicant, qualified representative or Minnesota manager for a PRIVATE DETECTIVE license must provide documentation supporting a minimum of 6,000 hours of employment, as an investigator in one or more of the following areas, showing competency and ability:

1. Employed as an investigator with a licensed private detective agency.
2. Employed as an investigator with a United States government investigative service.
3. Employed as an investigator for a city police department or sheriff's office.
4. Be employed in an occupation that the Board would find to be equivalent in scope, responsibility and training as one of the specific occupations listed above.

Each of the above qualification areas must be in line with dictates of Board rules.

EXPERIENCE—The applicant, qualified representative or Minnesota manager for a PROTECTIVE AGENT license must provide documentation supporting a minimum of 6,000 hours of employment in one or more of the following areas, showing competency and ability:

1. Employed in a protective/security capacity with a licensed protective agent, or in a protective/security, or investigative capacity for a licensed private detective. Subject is to have demonstrated experience in security systems, audits and supervision.
2. Employed in a protective/security capacity or as an investigator with a United States government investigative service.

3. Employed in a protective/security capacity, or as an investigator with a city police department or sheriff's office.

4. Be employed in an occupation that the Board would find upon review to be equivalent in scope, responsibility and training to one of the specific occupations listed above.

Each of the above qualification areas must be in line with dictates of Board rules.

The application package is provided by the Board once requested, and it first determines which license is being applied for, and what level of license is being sought (individual, partnership or corporation).

Minnesota statute outlines an application and qualification process for licensing. There is no testing requirement presently included in this process. Once an application package has been received, a required 20 day posting period occurs. This is a public announcement that a particular individual or business has made application.

Each person signing the application (i.e. Qualified Representative, Applicant, Minnesota Manager, Chief Executive Officer, Chief Financial Officer, Partner) must comply with the following:

1. Complete appropriate application forms (with appropriate signatures).

2. Complete a criminal history request form.

3. Submit a recent photograph and a full set of fingerprints.

4. Provide five references (not related by blood or marriage) who have known the subject for a minimum of five years.

5. The Qualified Representative and/or Minnesota

121

Manager must provide documentation or work experience (as outlined).

An application should be submitted to the Board's administrative office at: 1246 University Avenue, St. Paul, MN 55104.

Any questions can be addressed to the Board's Director, Marie Ohman at (612) 642-0775.

LICENSE FEE SCHEDULE

All applications must be accompanied by a nonrefundable application fee of $15.00.

License Fees are as follows:

PRIVATE DETECTIVE:
Individual	$500.00
Partnership	$850.00
Corporation	$950.00

PROTECTIVE AGENT:
Individual	$400.00
Partnership	$800.00
Corporation	$900.00

10

Beyond the Badge

This chapter comprises comments by ordinary people in the field of law enforcement and security—and their families.

"My dad was on the force for six years. At the end before he left, he was really stressed out. I remember one Christmas day in 1986 there was a shoot-out at a gas station downtown. His partner was shot and killed by a guy who robbed the place of $44. The killing was senseless, and Dad never got over it. His partner was also his best friend.

"I know the cops expect the worst to happen when they walk in to break up a roberry or murder attempt. They're prepared for it. But I don't think anyone is ever prepared when the worst actually happens. It takes everyone by surprise and leaves scars that last forever."

"I've been in traffic enforcement about three years now. It's a good job, and I like my work. I deal with ticketing vehicles for sign violations and meters and zone-stopping. I also oversee tow-away warnings.

"I've heard just about every excuse in the book. Older women have propositioned me to get out of a ticket. I've seen grown men cry. I've been threatened, lied to, and offered bribes. Sometimes I wonder, you know, it's only a ticket. But the stories that people come up with never cease to amaze me."

"Drug trafficking is not done out in the open. When dealers are out selling, they usually hide the stash somewhere and keep small amounts on them. That way if they get caught, the case usually won't go through the courts. It's tough, because I know what the real story is. I'm on to their activities. But the burden of proof is on me, and sometimes those dealers are let off free because there is a lack of evidence. Sometimes you get lucky and sometimes you don't."

"When I started at the police academy, I was proud that I had made it through the hiring process to become a police officer. I finally earned the needed credits, and my application was accepted. I took and passed the exam. The past few years have been good ones. I have many friends on the force and have been able to serve on different jobs in our community.

"There was a time when I thought the job was too much for me. I was involved in a heavy arrest situation and was shot twice in the right shoulder. I was ready to walk away, but later I learned that the guy I eventually arrested had been terrorizing kids. I received thank-yous from lots of people for helping to put the guy away. I guess in each of us there is something that keeps us going as cops."

"In my eight years with the New York police I have worked on a number of different assignments. The ones that get to me the most are the domestic violence calls. I may spend three hours trying to settle a fight where a boyfriend has bloodied his girlfriend's face. Black eyes, broken nose, the works. The time I spend is not getting him away from her, but trying to persuade her to press charges. She's afraid of what might happen to him and she's trying to protect him. After all he's done to her, it ends up being me that they're mad at. I sometimes wonder what makes people think and act the way they do. I can handle drug arrests and homicides and the worst of cases, but getting involved in domestic disputes is to me the toughest part of this job."

"My wife works vice in the Miami district. I worry about her because of all the crazies out there. She sometimes works as a decoy in the worst parts of town, you know, trying to flush the bad guys out of their hiding places. Pimps and prostitutes approach her, and she makes arrests on the spot. She gets involved in drug busts and has many close calls.

"Even though her job puts her in dangerous positions, she says she loves the work. She says that she never knows when a routine assignment will turn into an exciting challenge. She loves getting the bad guys. I have to admit that I'm proud of my wife. I worry about her all the time, but the honors she has received and the respect she has from her colleagues make me feel that she's really doing her job, and a good one at that."

"I work as a police diver. My specialty is retrieving bodies that for one reason or another have ended up at

125

the bottom of a body of water. The work is different and can sometimes be gruesome.

"I've had to search for murder victims whose bodies have been under water for weeks. The ocean diving is the easiest, I think. Swamps are the worst. In swamps, my enemies are alligators and snakes. In the ocean it's the sharks. Our lakes are simple to work in, but the pollution is getting worse each year. I feel that I really earn my pay."

"My husband, Gary, was a Highway Patrol man back in Missouri. We've been divorced for years, but sometimes it seems like yesterday. The first thing I want to say is that I was married to an officer who had a lot of integrity. That I was proud of. I know that he never took a bribe, he never took anything under the table. It happens a lot, but I would like to credit the people who are honest.

"Gary and I raised dogs, bloodhounds. They were ours, but they were also used by the Patrol. On Thanksgiving one year we got a phone call from a woman who was missing her husband. He had been gone forty-eight hours, and they found his car out in the woods. We were just about to sit down to a big dinner, but Gary left immediately and went out with the bloodhounds.

As it turned out, the woman's husband happened to change cars. He got into another car with a woman he had been seeing. When those things happen you get angry. You think, Gee—it should have been something important."

Emil Soorani is a board-certified psychiatrist in Santa Monica, California. He writes:

126

"I have been working with law enforcement officers from various walks of life—the regular police officer, the deputy sheriff, Secret Service, and parole officers. Even prison guards. My practice is medical/legal, and I work with affective disorders. I get referrals of injured police officers—some injured physically, others chemically.

"The stresses in police work are manyfold. One is the bureaucratic stress created by the hierarchy of the police department. Police departments are answerable to cities; cities have changes in administration that put pressure on the chiefs; chiefs put pressure on the captains, who put pressure on the men. And these pressures, that sometimes do not make sense, filter down to the men and women, and they feel it. Pressure in negotiating contracts is stressful. Sometimes the officers involved in negotiations are really harassed.

"One of my former patients had to leave the area and move to a different town. He was able to maintain his rank, but he became the enemy of the city. Sometimes the administrative pressure is as great or greater than the pressure out on the street.

"The beat officers have various pressures: boredom, threats to life, shootings, and witnessing other people's death in car accidents, homicides, and suicides.

"The memory of these incidents cannot escape the officer, it keeps working at the defenses. At some point or other the officer may crack, depending on how much stress he or she has been exposed to over the years.

"Often it is the family that becomes seriously affected by the stress that the officer brings home. The officer may have trouble sleeping, or become distant. Some try to escape pressure by drinking or having an affair.

"There is often a sense of peer pressure when it comes to drinking: If you don't drink you are not one of the guys or gals.

"Many officers like the respect and the power that come with the job. You do have a lot of power, but as with physicians, people expect too much of you and you expect too much of yourself. You start expecting that you should be a superman, but we all have our limits. We get tired, and officers are exposed to too many deaths, too many dead children. Dead children especially take a great toll on police officers. Overexposure to these situations can cause the officer to develop a chronic posttraumatic stress disorder. All of us need to ignore and suppress the fact that we are going to die, but if you are continuously exposed to it you begin to realize your vulnerability, your mortality. Thus, all kinds of symptoms of posttraumatic stress disorder come into play.

"It may take just one instance, or it may take years. The smarter police officers come forward and say that something is going on; the ones who are more guarded will hide it until they crack up.

"The police departments and the sheriff's departments have psychology departments, but they have their shortcomings. Many men and women fear that the psychologists and psychiatrists working for the department cannot be trusted. Counselors from the outside are more trusted. The men and women feel more comfortable with them because they feel they can open up a little more. I may tell them to retire, but I can do so without their feeling threatened: I'm not doing it to fire them, I'm doing it to help.

"I also work with Secret Service people, many of whom are former cops. The ones who are chosen for Secret Service are really tough, very bright people, men and women, high functioning, high I.Q., good record, very tough people.

"There is a lot of stress, many hours of work, a lot of traveling. They experience marital problems, separation

128

from their families, moving around, a lot of glamour. There is also the outside chance to have an affair.

"I work with law-enforcement officers who have problems, both alcohol and depression problems. Many times depression is not recognized until it is very late. I like to work with these guys, to help and lecture in this area. I have been working with police officers from almost every single department since 1982."

11

Planning Your Career

In previous chapters we talked about the many opportunities available within the law-enforcement and security field. After reading about the requirements and qualifications that each job entails, you should have a better understanding of how and where you should begin to make the necessary preparations.

Most jobs in this field require that you take courses that will familiarize you with the work. You can begin by taking high school elective courses such as civics or political science. You will also be required to go through a training period, pass a written or oral examination, or both.

The more specialized careers, such as FBI and Secret Service, require more before you are even considered for the job. Investigators will dig deep into your background and look closely at all aspects of your past and present life. Besides honesty and a desire to work, they will be looking for a law-abiding citizen with a clear record.

Employers are continuously on the lookout for hard-working, trustworthy individuals who have a strong desire to succeed in the job. A good employee is a reflection upon the company or organization that hires him or her.

Perhaps you have always wanted to become a police

officer. You remember dreaming of wearing a badge and uniform and proudly serving on the force. Now, as you're approaching the middle or upper grades of school, the time to make that decision is growing closer. As you near graduation, a definite plan of action must be initiated. There are courses to sign up for and applications to fill out. There are interviews to go on and new people to meet. You must start thinking about your plans for the future and what direction to take.

Listen closely to the advice from those who contributed to this book. Try to remember what was said about police work; about security guards and detectives. Security guards do face some degree of danger in their job, and Secret Service agents often spend a great deal of time traveling and away from their families. But as most who are working in law enforcement and security agree, the rewards far outweigh the drawbacks. If you choose this career you will be responsible for protecting society against thieves, criminals, and other undesirables wishing to harm others. Some of you will be credited with saving lives.

Think how it must feel to be prepared to give up your own life to protect the President of the United States. Or to find a missing child and bring her back to a grateful family. You may be the one who saves a company millions of dollars because of your watchful eye.

The field of law enforcement and security is an important and gratifying career choice, one that has many opportunities just waiting for the right people. Perhaps you are that person. Start by choosing a field that interests you and read all the information you can find about it. Talk to people who are already working in the job. It is never too early to start preparing.

Rudolf Kies, PhD, is a former intelligence officer. He worked as a criminal investigator and was once a deputy sheriff in Lincoln, Nebraska. Kies served as

131

a consultant to local, national, and international investigative agencies throughout the years. Currently he is Director of Kies Intelligence Agency. The authors asked Mr. Kies to contribute his thoughts and feelings about working in the law-enforcement field, and he wrote the following:

A Career in Law Enforcement

"Of course, as law enforcement goes, unless one spends a number of years in this type of work, it is extremely difficult to picture or predict a life-style involved with the darker side of human nature. Or is it the darker side?

"We all commit crimes. As one criminal justice professor once put it, we cheat—well, just a little—on taxes, we run an occasional red light, we should put some money in that parking meter from time to time, and so on. But that doesn't make me a criminal, you say. And you are right, it doesn't. Still, the percentage of people with a 'criminal mind' is very low in our society today, thanks to good law enforcement and good social teaching.

"'But then what's the point,' you lament, 'if I can't become a cop and chase real criminals and feel the thrill of the danger involved in this type of work?' Well, in some areas around the country there isn't any work involved in being a cop, or so it seems. But don't forget, chasing criminals is only half of the picture. The other half, of course, is helping people in a plain old-fashioned way. How? Well, if you're a young man thinking of becoming a police officer, think back to when you were a little toddler crossing the street or looking for your dog or riding your bicycle the wrong way.

"You may say 'Gosh, that's not what I want! That's stupid!' Not at all. Police work is an education in itself, and it will take you as far as your ability allows you to go. It is perhaps the only professional field that allows one to enter as a young man, attend some police academy, and after a while continue to improve your education and work performance and 'work your way up.'

"The difficult part in planning one's career, of course, is to know ahead of time just what to expect of oneself, say, ten, twenty years down the road. To attend college and take all the Administration of Justice courses available is a sure way to find recognition in law enforcement. On the other hand, police work is composed of many specialties. Intelligence is one such special field.

"Intelligence? Yes! But let's differentiate between police intelligence and the kind you hear about on the evening news. Police intelligence involves the kind of information-gathering that is related to the commission of a crime, or the prevention of one, such as murder, arson, or burglary. Police intelligence is necessary to plan a safe environment for the population, to enable to leaders of a community to prevent large-scale crimes such as dealing in drugs or narcotics.

"But there are other forms of intelligence. On the federal level, of course, we are not so much concerned with the commission or prevention of crime as with the kind of information needed to protect our Constitution and to prevent the erosion and subversion of our basic rights. Those are the true guardians of our freedom!

"Though basically a law enforcement agency, the FBI is most widely known in that category. The Mann Act, the Deyer Act, the Interstate Commerce Act. 'Hold it right there!' you scream. That's OK, you'll learn all about them if you join that special group. You have to have graduated from law school or be an accounant, if that's where your interests lie.

"Central Intelligence Agency. 'What do I need? How do I get in? Whom do I see? How do I prepare?' Well, as for the first question, nothing really. Nothing? Well, some good basic education plus a specialty currently in demand. Something like electronics, a language or two, and a major in psychology. Ethnic or cultural background and specialty education are the things that will open the doors for you there. More than that, they will take the doors off the hinges for you. Your college recruiter is the person to see if that's the kind of life that interests you most. As an intelligence officer your primary goal is to identify, predict, and possibly modify criminal or subversive behavior.

"Not all intelligence work is exciting. In fact, very little of it is in terms of public recognition. You are totally submerged in some profession, some activity not associated with what you are actually doing. However, personal satisfaction comes with accumulating life experiences and relationships with people of different origins, but most of all, in the knowledge that you are doing a job that few are able to do. For the broader-minded young student I would wholeheartedly recommend a career in government intelligence.

"So, you see, the difference between the various intelligence agencies is not really that great. They all have different objectives, and their activities are geared to accomplish that objective. Consequently, your role as an agent, or your life-style as an agent, is influenced by the broader goal of the agency that employs you. That is to say, if you want to stay in one place, want close contact with people on a daily basis, your local police department is the right choice. If, on other hand, you want travel and activity on a national level, still fighting crime, then the FBI is your future. But if you are the quiet type, one who observes rather than being observed; one who remains in the background but enjoys a mentally and emotionally stimulating life while performing some technical or specialty occupation; one who needs the fulfilling assurance of making a real contribution to the stability of our world, I can only suggest that some form of intelligence work may be the right environment for you."

For Further Reading

Book

Anderberg, Nadin. *The First Official Law Enforcement Cookbook*. Saratoga, CA: R & E Publishers Inc., 1993.

Law Enforcement Employment Guide. Mt. Shasta, CA: Lawman Press, 1990.

McAlary, Mike. *Buddy Boys: When Good Cops Turn Bad*. New York: Putman, 1987.

Nadelmann, Ethan A. *Cops Across Borders: The Internationalization of U.S. Law Enforcement*. University Park: Pennsylvania State University Press, 1993.

Rush, George. *Confessions of an Ex-Secret Service Agent: The Marty Venker Story*. New York: Donald Fine, 1988.

Schmalleger, Frank. *Criminal Justice: A Brief Introduction*. Englewood Cliffs, NJ: Prentice-Hall, 1994.

Steinberg, E.P. *Law Enforcement Exams Handbook*. Englewood Cliffs, NJ: Prentice-Hall General Reference, 1993.

Warner, John W. *Federal Jobs in Law Enforcement*. Englewood Cliffs, NJ: Prentice-Hall General Reference, 1992.

Woodward, Bob. *The Secret Wars of the CIA*. New York: Simon & Schuster, 1987.

Articles

Broussard, Ginger. "I'm a Miami Vice Cop." *Good Housekeeping*, October 1986.

Dounham, Parker Barss. "Inferno on Queen Street." *Reader's Digest* (Canadian), December 1987.

Snowden, Lynn. "Blues in the Night." *Interview*, August 1988.

Urbanska, Wanda. "I Like to Get the Bad Guys." *McCall's*, February 1989.

Index